FAN THE FLAME

*Living Out
Your First Love
for Christ*

JOSEPH M. STOWELL

All Scripture quotations, unless otherwise noted, are taken from the *Holy
Bible: New International Version*. Copyright © 1973, 1978, 1984 by the International Bible Society. Used by permission of Zondervan Bible Publishers.

Library of Congress Cataloging in Publication Data

Stowell, Joseph M.
    Fan the flame.

    1. Christian life—Baptist authors.   I. Title.
BV4501.2.S794   1986   248.4   86-12794
ISBN 0-8024-2528-3 (pbk.)

5 6 Printing/BC/Year 91 90 89 88

Printed in the United States of America

With deep love
and thanksgiving
for my wife,
Martie,
whose gracious gift of discernment
has been a purifying force in my life

Acknowledgments

I am gratefully indebted to:

Martie,

whose life, example, and partnership provide
strength to carry on;

Joseph,
Elisabeth,
and Matthew,

whose patience with their daddy's deadlines
encouraged me;

Monalee Ferrero,

whose secretarial skills and insightful input
helped process the manuscript;

David Borror,
David Carder,
Kenneth Hall,
Gary Matthews,
John Orme,
David Sheaffer,
and Donald Woodworth,

whose partnership in ministry
releases me to study and write;

and
the flock of God
at the Highland Park Baptist Church,

whose vision for a ministry to the Body of Christ at large
makes a book like this possible.

*I thank my God every time I remember you. In all my prayers
for all of you, I always pray with joy because of your partnership in the gospel from the first day until now, being confident
of this, that he who began a good work in you will carry it on
to completion until the day of Christ Jesus.*

—Philippians 1:3-6

Contents

CHAPTER   PAGE

1. Heartstyle: 11
    Authentic Christianity

2. Christ at the Core: 23
    Fanning the Flame

3. Life-style: 35
    Living It Out

4. Rules in Perspective: 49
    Codes or Principles

5. Loving God: 61
    The Principle of Surrender

6. Loving God: 71
    The Principle of Templing

7. Loving Our Neighbor: 83
    The Principle of True Love

8. Loving Our Neighbor: 93
    The Principle of Otherness

9. Excellence: 107
    The Principle of Choices

10. Guaranteed to Last: 119
    The Principle of the Kingdom

11. Inside-Out Righteousness: 131
    Application

1

Heartstyle:
Authentic Christianity

Blind?

The doctor was talking about our three-year-old son, Matthew. We could hardly believe what we heard. It seemed so unlikely. So serious. So sad. "Without surgery and corrective glasses," our doctor continued, "his eye will become functionally blind." He called it "atrophy," which is what happens when an organ becomes useless due to disuse.

Atrophy is not only a physical problem; it is an ever-present danger in our relationship to Christ as well. Spiritual atrophy strikes the heart. If not nourished and nurtured, our hearts become cold to Christ and spiritually dysfunctional, leaving us with a Christianity that is hollow, habitual, and even hypocritical. A spiritual experience that was once an inward joy can become no more than a way of life—at times even a burden. Spiritual atrophy deadens the enthusiasm, spontaneity, and zeal of our Christian experience.

I recently caught a glimpse of the Statue of Liberty from an airplane window. To my surprise she was surrounded by 300,000 feet of scaffolding. I watched briefly as workmen cleaned, scraped, welded and polished her surface. The image of the scaffolded statue riveted itself to my mind. Why did she need all the external support? Her problem was that she was a hollow lady. She had no heart; she had to rely on external forces to maintain her. I thought, *How many of us are just like that, with hearts deadened through years of disuse?* We live our Christianity reliant on the scaffolding we have built around us. We count on pastors and friends to maintain us. Books, tapes, articles, traditions, parents scurry around our scaffolding, keeping us mended, polished, and pure. As good as each of those may be, we have let them do all our spiritual work for us. And we like the statue are hollow, with little or no vibrancy at the heart level.

We become like chocolate Easter bunnies. We look good—sweet and alluring—but we are fragile. Don't press too hard! Under the pressure of trials, temptations, and unexpected crises we may fold.

The great cathedrals of Europe intrigue me. Because their massive ceilings were too heavy for the walls to support, gothic architects built flying buttresses—external extensions to support the expansive roofs. We too are cathedrals, temples of the living God. Yet we are prone to live out our faith by the flying buttresses of a dozen good but external influences while we remain weak at the core.

Authentic Christianity

If we have not yet learned that authentic Christianity is a matter of being strong from the inside out, that it is first and foremost a matter of heart condition, then we have missed the whole point of our walk with Christ and will be vulnerable to a host of spiritual dangers.

Why would a student fall spiritually his first year away from home? Perhaps he lived by the scaffolding of parental pressure, having little first-hand personal experience with God. Why would a deacon pull the shades and entertain himself with immoral cable or video material? Why would someone play fantasy games in his mind where no one else could see?

Why would one get tired of his Christianity? Why would right-eousness become boring? All those things can happen when our Christianity loses heart.

Instead of growing deeper and richer at the center, we tend to grow more shallow, more hollow. We maintain our exteriors, but we become poorer on the inside.

Let's face it. It is easier to live by the scaffolding. But opting for the easy way means losing the most significant aspect of our Christian experience: a heart for God. It is a heart for God that produces joy, spontaneity, intimacy, and strength. We must remember that the heart is where God meets and relates to us. If our hearts are cold toward Him, then we have lost the essence of our Christian experience. In fact, a cold heart soon becomes a carnal heart. Sin is always waiting, ready to move into hearts that have ceased to intimately relate to Christ. Is it any wonder that God's Word says, "Above all else, guard your heart, for it is the wellspring of life" (Proverbs 4:23)?

HEARTSTYLE

What is the nature of this place where the flames of spiritual intimacy must burn? *Heart* is used in Scripture as the most comprehensive term for the authentic person. It is the part of our being where we desire, deliberate, and decide. It has been described as "the place of conscious and decisive spiritual activity," "the comprehensive term for a person as a whole: his feelings, desires, passions, thought, understanding and will," and "the center of a person. The place to which God turns."

Christ graphically and repeatedly points out that God is primarily concerned about our interior. In fact, in both the Old and New Testaments it is clear that God measures us at the heart level. It is interesting to note that Christ pounded this truth home in the midst of a religious atmosphere that was very concerned about external righteousness. The Pharisees had a neatly tailored life-style, but as Christ so dramatically said, they were like "whitewashed tombs" (Matthew 23:27), externally pure but dead at the core.

It convicts me to discover that God is concerned about my heartstyle. Heartstyle must precede life-style. Yet life-style remains the primary concern of many Christians. It is easier to emphasize behavior rather than character. External systems of habit, heritage, and ritual buttress us until we become like high-tech spiritual robots.

In the Old Testament God denounces Israel for hitchhiking on externals. Though outwardly circumcised He called them "uncircumcised in heart" (Jeremiah 9:26; cf. 4:4), and in another text He told them to repent by rending their hearts and not their garments (Joel 2:13).

God told King Asa that He searches for hearts that are singularly loyal to Him that He might empower them in a special way (2 Chronicles 16:1-9). That statement was a reproof to Asa whose heart had been disloyal to God. God was not impressed with his status as king. He went right for Asa's heart and found it wanting.

I have been a pastor for fifteen years. That is not long, but as a pastor I have done many things on God's behalf. As He inspects my life I would like to tell Him how many times I have proclaimed His Word, how many people have been married, buried, helped, saved, and have grown in grace under my care.

But He is not impressed. He moves past all of that and tests my heart.

As He approaches your life, you might be tempted to stop Him and flash your business card. After all, it's not every day He gets a corporate executive on His team. He is not impressed.

You may remind Him that you have taught Sunday school for forty-six years and that you are going to make it to fifty. He's not impressed.

"But wait, Lord, my son is a missionary." "I serve on the boards of two Christian organizations." "I've stuck with my church through thick and thin." He steps by all of that and goes right for the heart.

I like David's transparency. He opens his life to a spiritual EKG. How significant to hear him pray, "Search me, O God, and know my heart; test me and know my anxious thoughts. See if there is any offensive way in me, and lead me in the way everlasting" (Psalm 139:23-24).

HEARTMEASURE

What kind of heart does God look for? What are the signs of atrophy? How can we know if the flame has died, if carnality has captured our heart? God measures our hearts by at least six standards.

LOYALTY

In 2 Chronicles 16:1-9 we have the story of King Asa's last days, when his loyalty to the Lord was tested. The seer Hanani reproved Asa because he had been disloyal to God by striking an allegiance with the pagan king Ben-hadad. Israel had attacked Judah, and now the king of Judah was surrounded and overpowered.

His options? Remain loyal to God by trusting Him for deliverance in the face of great danger. After all, God had helped His children many times against great military odds.

Or, he could pay Ben-hadad and his army to supply deliverance. It would mean taking money from the temple treasury. It would mean that God's people would be aligned with a godless nation. It would say in essence that the God of Judah was too weak to protect and deliver His people. But then, it seemed to be the most expedient, the most practical and efficient way to handle the problem. So Asa struck the deal.

God then said to Asa, "The eyes of the Lord range throughout the earth to strengthen those whose hearts are fully committed to him. You have done a foolish thing, and from now on you will be at war" (v.9).

Our hearts show themselves when life puts us in a bind. When there is too much month left at the end of the money, do we backtrack on our stewardship responsibilities or remain loyal by trusting Him to provide? Would we strike a less than honest business deal to pad a paycheck? Would we be disloyal to our Lord by lying our way out of a tight spot? Most girls would like someday to be married. Any girl worth her stuff has a list of qualifications: a believer with strong spiritual commitments; responsible; kind; sensitive; athletic; fun loving; serious at the right times. At least twenty qualities could fill the list of a nineteen-year-old woman in waiting. But a strange thing happens when she is thirty-five and still single. The list is reduced to two: warm and breathing. What would we do if our "last" chance to get married were with an unsaved person?

Our true heart condition is demonstrated by whether or not we are loyal to God when the chips are down.

Dan was in a bind. As an upwardly mobile executive in a cable TV company he was transferred to our area to manage its operation. He had a lucrative career with a bright future. As he grew in the Lord he began to realize that selling some of the programming of his company to the homes in our area was in direct conflict with his commitment to righteousness.

He decided to step off the corporate ladder. He resigned. He wanted to be.loyal to His God.

He had nowhere to go, but he decided to trust in God.

As he moved back to family in Minneapolis I thought, *He left town with his heart showing.* In the face of great odds he maintained his loyalty to God.

TREASURES

Christ sees our heart condition reflected in what we do with our treasures. He taught, "Do not store up for yourselves treasures on earth, where moth and rust destroy, and where thieves break in and steal. But store up for yourselves treasures in heaven, where moth and rust do not destroy, and where thieves do not break in and steal. For where your treasure is, there your heart will be also" (Matthew 6:19-21). In essence He says, If you are wondering where your heart is, you will find it where your treasures are.

I can tell a lot about your heart by the way you read the newspaper. If you pick up the morning news and go right for the sports section, I know your heart. If you are interested in current events, it is the front page. Finances? The stock page. Is life driving you insane? The comics.

God can tell our heart condition by where we put our treasures. I do not know about you, but my treasures are my wife, my children, friends, time, money and my house.

In these verses Christ indicates that there are two treasure chests: the chest of temporal, earthly gain and the chest of eternal value.

How do I spend my time? Do I manage my day to invest my time for things of eternal value? Is my money used for His glory, to advance His kingdom? Would I encourage my children to pursue careers in Christian ministry, or would I rather they be doctors and lawyers?

THOUGHTS

The mind is the ultimate in personal privacy. It is that safe corner that no one can invade. As a result we tend to be very much ourselves in our minds. We can relax. We do not have to put up a front to impress anyone. This is where immoral fantasies and schemes can be played out in minute detail. Thoughts of revenge, jealousy, hatred, lingering anger, and envy can have full range in our minds. Christ said that our thoughts reflect our hearts. "Why do you entertain evil thoughts in your heart?" was His reproof to the Pharisees (Matthew 9:4).

A good heart reflects thoughts that are pure, peaceful, forgiving, and loving. It is no wonder Paul said, "Whatever is true, whatever is noble, whatever is right, whatever is pure, whatever is lovely, whatever is admirable—if anything is excellent or praiseworthy—think about such things" (Philippians 4:8).

Solomon warned, "As he thinketh in his heart, so is he" (Proverbs 23:7, KJV*).

WORDS

Christ said, "Out of the overflow of the heart the mouth speaks" (Matthew 12:34). The tongue is the tattletale of the heart.

I have often been with people whose words are telling on their hearts. I feel like saying, "Stop! Your heart is showing." There have been times, more than I would like to admit, when words have passed my lips that I would have liked to grab and jam back in because my heart was showing.

In Proverbs we read, "A wise man's heart guides his mouth, and his lips promote instruction" (Proverbs 16:23).

RESPONSE TO THE WORD

In Christ's parable of the sower, He states that the good soil responds to God's word by hearing, retaining, and producing through His Word. Luke says the good soil is "a noble and good heart" (Luke 8:15).

Our hearts are measured by how well we respond to the Word of God. I recognize that there are some who have intentionally hardened their hearts against His Word. I am sure that some walk into our congregations having said to themselves, *I don't care what is said; God is not going to change my life.* Some have chained and padlocked portions of their hearts and in essence have told God, *That's off limits.*

Some listen to the Word as though they had giant reflectors in front of their hearts. As the Word approaches them they think, *That's just what Barbara needs to hear,* or *I hope my wife is listening.*

They then point their reflectors towards the other person and bounce the Word in that direction.

* King James Version.

A good heart takes the Word personally. It comes to the Word with a funnel, not a reflector. It hears the Word, retains it, and produces a crop through it. Any short-circuiting of that three-phase process defeats the purpose of God's Word. It takes discipline to hear the Word; keeping our minds from wandering is hard work. It takes honesty to hear the Word; we must admit that we are what it says we are. It takes diligence to retain the Word—journal; notebook; memorization; review. It amazes me that I can remember sleazy little rhymes and sayings from my childhood in an instant yet forget a verse I memorized last month. Satan has a great way of jamming in all that is bad and pulling the plug on the significant. A good heart then produces a crop. God's Word was not intended to make us smart or theologically astute. It was intended to change us, to produce the fruit of righteousness, the image of Christ, in and through our lives.

A heart is measured by its response to the Word.

WORSHIP

Among Christ's most stinging reproofs to the Pharisees was his quote of Isaiah: "These people honor me with their lips, but their hearts are far from me" (Matthew 15:8). The Pharisees prayed, praised, and proclaimed in worship to God with their lips. But, as Christ points out in this text, their clinging to personal and false traditions demonstrated that their hearts were far from God.

We pastors are in a unique position to watch people worship on Sunday morning. Many have come to worship our true and living God, but I periodically notice other attitudes displayed. A few, while preparing for the awesome privilege of worship, see an activity in the bulletin that they do not like. They turn to their neighbor: "Did you see what the youth department is doing? We would have never done that when I was growing up."

Then the leader calls them to worship: "Let us all turn to

hymn forty-two, 'Amazing Grace,' and lift our voices to our gracious Savior."

They sigh and reach for the hymnals. *What was that number again? "Amazing Grace"? We sang that three weeks ago. Why don't they pick something else?*

"Let us stand as we worship Him."

Stand! Why do we have to stand?

"We will sing all four stanzas."

All four stanzas! Why not sing one and get on with it?

The lips move as they sing but the heart is far from Him.

Then comes the pastoral prayer. I once had a deacon who would time my pastoral prayers. At the deacon's meeting he would report the length and denounce the fact that we spent too much time in prayer.

Then the Word of God is proclaimed. Sermon time, and they start dropping like flies. Twenty minutes into it and someone is checking his watch to see why it stopped. At noon all the wristwatch alarms start to go off.

Our worship traditions say a lot about our heart condition.

I think there must be times when God weeps at 11:00 A.M. on Sunday.

Spiritual EKGs

God measures us at the heart level. Externals are only symptomatic, superficial, and cosmetic. Externally we can fool all the people most of the time. But God? Never!

I was preparing to go into the evening service one Sunday night when I heard that Bob, my friend and a deacon in the church, had just collapsed on the sidewalk. As I approached, the emergency unit pulled up, and three medical technicians jumped out. Did they attempt to rearrange his motionless body? Did they straighten his tie? Did they comb his hair and polish his shoes?

Not on your life. It was no time for cosmetics. They went right for the heart. That was the crux of the matter.

God goes right for the heart. It is where He meets us. It is where He evaluates us. It is where He desires that the flame of an intimate, life-changing relationship with Him be fanned into a great source of spiritual heat and light. He desperately seeks to dwell with us at the core. As Christ said, "Behold, I stand at the door, and knock; if any man hear my voice, and open the door, I will come in to him, and will sup with him, and he with me" (Revelation 3:20, KJV).

The call of authentic Christianity is to "have a heart"—a heart for God. A heart for God requires that we move from externals to internals, that we reject the easy way of ritual and habit. It requires that we develop a vibrant relationship with Christ at the very core of our being.

2

Christ at the Core:
Fanning the Flame

He was twenty-five and had already captured the hearts of Russia with his novel *Poor Folk*. Fame quickly went to his head. He drank immoderately and partied wildly. He carelessly criticized the Czarist regime.

You did not do that in Czarist Russia.

He was arrested in St. Petersburg and sentenced to death by the firing squad along with several other dissidents.

It was a cold December morning. Dressed in a white execution gown, he was led to the wall of the prison courtyard with the others. Blindfolded, he waited for the last sound he would hear, the crack of a pistol echoing off the prison walls. Instead he heard fast paced footsteps; then the announcement that the Czar had commuted his sentence to ten years of hard labor.

So intense was that moment that he suffered an epileptic seizure, something he would live with the rest of his life.

In that Siberian prison Fyodor Dostoevsky was allowed only a New Testament to read. There he discovered something more wonderful, more true than his socialistic ideals. He met Christ, and his heart was changed. Upon leaving prison he wrote to a friend who had helped him grow in Christ,

To believe that there is nothing more beautiful, more profound, more sympathetic, more reasonable, more manly and
more perfect than Christ. And not only is there nothing but I
tell myself with jealous love that there can be nothing. Be-
sides, if anyone proved to me that Christ was outside the
truth and it really was so that the truth was outside Christ,
then I would prefer to remain with Christ, than with the
truth.

Dostoevsky returned to civilian life. He wrote feverishly and
produced his prison memories, *The House of the Dead,* and
then *Crime and Punishment,* followed by many other major
works.

Yet His church attendance was sporadic, and he never grew
as a Christian. He neglected Bible study and the fellowship of
other believers. No Christian took him under his wing to disciple him. He began to drink. He gambled. Excessive drinking
and compulsive gambling unraveled his life so that he died
penniless and wasted. He left prison with his flame lit for
Christ and died with nothing more than smoldering embers.

The tragedy of Fyodor Dostoevsky is not so much what he
became but what he could have become for Christ. In the
words of the poet, "of all sad words of tongue or pen, the sad-
dest are these: 'It might have been.'"

PILGRIMS PLUNDERED

What happened to Dostoevsky is not unique. A strange thing
happens on our way from spiritual birth to heaven. Our pilgrimage gets plundered by the loss of that fresh, first love for
Christ. Not all go to the depths of Dostoevsky's devastation,
but for all of us the flame is prone to flicker.

I can remember early in my ministry talking with my wife
about never wanting to become "professional" in my work for
Christ. I sensed that some pastors were doing their duty without much devotion. Funerals, weddings, and sermons seemed
to be professionally performed. I thought, *I never want to lose*

my heart for Christ's work. Now, fifteen years later, after hundreds of funerals, weddings, counseling appointments, and messages, I find that the subtle drift toward professionalism and devotionless duty is a danger to me.

People often say to me, "Pastor, how do I recapture that fresh sense of vibrancy that I once had as a believer?" We have all seen people start out with a heart for God but soon settle in and let the fire die. I have often thought that there has to be a way to keep new believers from being around those who have traded a relationship with Christ for a religious routine. But I must remind myself that this pilgrimage is plundered from within and that all of us are vulnerable to having our vitality victimized, even if we never meet another believer.

Duty Does Not Count

We deceive ourselves when we assume that being busy "doing" for Christ is sufficient to please Him. The church at Ephesus provides a striking model as to what Christ thinks of our doing our duty void of devotion to Him. The Ephesians had an impressive list of duties that they performed, listed in Revelation 2:2-3, 6.

Deeds. In this age of grace we often discount the value of works. Though they do not save us, good works are the expression of genuine faith (James 2:14-19). They are the sacrifice from our lives that is pleasing to God (Hebrews 13:16). From Sunday school teaching to inner city ministry, our works are important to God.

Hard work. Spiritual work is often hard work. Some days it is hard to pray, to study, to witness, or to love. It takes spiritual muscle to do what is right. The Ephesians had this to their credit.

Perseverance. One of the highest qualities of our calling in Christ is to persevere and to not fold under pressure (Hebrews 12:1-2). The Ephesians had stick-to-it-iveness, and Christ complimented them for it.

Purity. The Ephesian believers refused to "tolerate wicked men," probably a reference to church discipline. They took a courageous step that is often overlooked in our churches today.

Doctrinal authenticity. They "tested" those who taught to see if they were genuinely fit for apostolic authority. They refused false teachers so that the truth might remain pure and that authority in the church would not be threatened.

Suffered well. Though hardships had come as a result of their faith in Christ, the Ephesians endured, and they refused to trade their commitment to Christianity for fleeting comfort and cultural acceptability.

Rejected immorality. The Nicolaitans lived licentiously while claiming to embrace Christianity. They were soft on immorality. The believers at Ephesus refused to excuse sensual behavior and took a clear stand for moral purity.

After all of those accolades I am ready to nominate this group for "Church of the Year."

Christ would veto the nomination. He says of them, "I hold this against you: You have forsaken your first love. . . . If you do not repent, I will come to you and remove your lampstand from its place" (Revelation 2:4-5).

In spite of all their faithfulness to duty, something was missing. They were not pleasing to God. Their behavior was blighted. Something had corroded their Christianity; their orthodoxy was faulty. Christ pointedly called them to repentance.

DEVOTION PRECEDES DUTY

Christ is concerned with more than what we do. He is initially concerned about why we do what we do. Christ wants our external activities to be produced out of a personal relationship with Him. He demands something deeper than habit, more significant than ritual, more delightful than duty for duty's sake.

When our children were babies, they brought some addi-

tional duties into our lives. Some pleasant, others more pain-
ful—like changing diapers. Why did I do diaper duty? Because
that's what fathers do? Because the child would stop crying if I
did? All of those may have been a part of it, but the greatest
joy in duty came when I did it because I cared about my wife
and wanted to express my love for her by doing something for
her.

Devotion adds delight to duty.

Christ speaks of devotion in terms of our "first love" (Revelation 2:4). The word "first" in this text refers to priority. It is
that to which everything else takes a subsequent, consequent,
dependent, or secondary status. The word "love" is the word
not for an emotional feeling but for a commitment, a yielding,
a surrendering to another. Our priority commitment, our point
of surrender upon which everything else is dependent or secondary, must be our commitment to Him.

A true Christian experience has its source in and is motivated by a personal relationship to Christ. Not just a personal
relationship that saves me, but a relationship that determines
my behavior, responses, thoughts, and actions in ways that
would be particularly pleasing to Him.

Christianity is first and foremost a determined devotion to
Christ. It is a Christ-centered experience. It is Christ at the
core. The Ephesians had denied that. For them Christ had become a corollary to their faith instead of the core of their faith.
They opted for ritual without relationship, and Christ called
them to repentance.

Living out my "first love" for Christ means striving to do
what I do, say what I say, think what I think, and respond the
way I respond because of my personal, internal relationship to
Christ. It is making Him the primary force, motivation, source,
and resource in my life. Because He is my ultimate priority, all
that I do is for Him and because of Him.

If Christ is my first love, then my behavior is not shaped by
who is watching, what makes me feel good, what my heritage
says, what I have always done, or what someone else expects

of me. Exercising my first love for Christ liberates me from the scaffolding and eliminates the flying buttresses. With Christ at the core I behave because of Him. I, husband and father, teach, preach, help, and play to please Him.

My daughter, Libby, is just now discovering boys. More frightening, boys are discovering her. The day may come when she will fall in love with one. At that point, all that she thinks, says, eats, buys, wears, and does will be because of him. Nothing else will matter.

If she marries him, life will work against keeping him at the core. There will be many distractions: children, a home to keep, perhaps a job, or even work at the church. So it is with our relationship to Christ. In the seductive environment of a busy materialistic age we tend to abandon our priority commitment to Christ. We continue to do, but it is no longer because of Him. We slowly and subtly lose our purpose on the inside.

THE SYSTEM OR THE SAVIOR

My friend Pat Williams, general manager of the Philadelphia Seventy-Sixers, writes of the erosion of his marriage in the book *Rekindled.** He recalls the intriguing way he and his wife, Jill, met. She was a beauty queen, and he was immersed in professional sports. They met, fell in love, and soon married. It was romance at its best.

By his own confession, Pat tells of a subtle shift that then began to take place in their lives. It was so subtle he did not even realize it was eroding the most precious thing to him —his relationship to Jill. Pat found great pride in his home and marriage. He would often tell people what a good a mother and homemaker Jill was. He reveled in the fact that he was free to be a success in his profession because of his wife's good work at home. She kept house, chauffeured the children,

* by Pat and Jill Williams with Jerry Jenkins (Old Tappan, N.J.: Revell, 1985).

cooked, and was his social companion. Without even knowing it, Pat was shifting from a vibrant relationship with his wife to a complacent involvement with the "institution of marriage," the organization called "home." He and Jill still talked, ate, and slept together, but they were losing the most important ingredient—the intimacy of their love for each other.

It is often that way in our relationship to Christ. We, in time, find ourselves more related to the *system* than to the *Savior.*

The systems are all around us. They are the things we used to do because of our devotion to Christ. Now we do them because we have always done them, because we are supposed to do them, because someone told us to do them or twisted our arm to do them, because we feel guilty if we don't do them, or because everyone else is doing them.

Systems.

Systems of teaching, doctrine, denominations, Bible reading, prayer, witnessing, preaching, counseling, committees, missions, boards, discipleship, note-taking, Christian vocabulary, conferences, camping, reading, taping, attending, and participating.

Duties. Functions. Activities.

All of it is good and admirable—yet scarred, because it has become ritual without relationship, duty without devotion, smoke but no fire.

Analysis

If a flame is flickering, there is a reason: not enough oxygen, too much moisture, lack of combustible material. Christ told the Ephesians that their flame went out because they had *"forsaken* their first love."

Note the sense of personal responsibility. They had not simply lost it; they had forsaken it, abandoned it.

The story recently appeared in our Detroit paper of a man who heard a strange noise while walking by a garbage dumpster. It sounded like a whimper; he stopped. It was a baby crying. He looked inside the dumpster, moved some trash, and there wrapped in a blanket was an infant—not lost, but abandoned by its mother.

When we find that we are more related to the system than the Savior, it is because we have abandoned our beginning. As subtle as the shift may be, we are responsible for the flickering flame.

It strikes me that the letter in Revelation 2 was written when the Ephesian church was in its second generation. Ritualism is especially prevalent in succeeding generations of Christians. I am a third-generation believer, a third-generation pastor. I have to ask myself, Why am I in this? Am I in it because of my priority commitment to Christ, or am I in it because it is all I have ever known? My life-style is my heritage. I was born and bred in it. It is comfortable—a known commodity. It has been culturally ingrained in me. I could live it with my eyes closed. I could live it without Christ at the core. I could live it by habit and not by heart.

Yet it remains my responsibility to fan the flame of what Christ called the "first love."

DANGER

One night, Jill told Pat that over a period of time something had happened to her love for him. The words pierced him like flaming arrows. She said, "Pat, I don't love you anymore. I'll stay with you because of the children, but my love for you is gone." He had lost the most precious treasure in his life.

When we do not exercise our devotion to Christ we stand to lose something very special. Christ put it this way: "If you do not repent, I will come to you and remove your lampstand from its place" (Revelation 2:5). Their light, their power, their effectiveness would be removed. It is as though Christ says that if we want empty, ritual, devotionless duty then we can have our ritual and duty, but it will indeed be empty and ineffective.

One thing that haunts me as a pastor is that somehow God might remove His hand of blessing from me. Powerless professionalism in the ministry is poverty in the ministry. As a father, husband, friend, and associate I want to be, more than anything else, effective for Christ and His kingdom.

In bed that night Pat was unable to sleep. Long after Jill had fallen asleep he lay there with tears moistening his pillow. All he could think about was what he had lost. Thoughts of those early days of love and vibrancy in their relationship haunted his bedroom. As he remembered the past he longed to have it back.

Christ said to the believers at Ephesus, "*Remember* the height from which you have fallen! *Repent* and do the things you did at first." Two steps are required in order to put Christ back at the core: we must contemplate what we have lost and we must change our patterns of behavior. It is significant that Christ says we have fallen from a high place. Duty without devotion is a low-level Christian experience. Christ calls on us to think carefully about what we have lost.

In the best sense of the phrase, reflecting on the "good old days" is the beginning of a new heart for God. Stop and visualize what it was like when Christ was at the center. Recall the joy of church, discovery, fellowship, and serving. Stop long enough to recollect those special days and you will ignite a desire to get it back.

There are some things we can never get back: our youth, young romance, high school fun. Remembering them is nothing more than nostalgia. But this is more than nostalgia because a priority commitment to Christ can be reclaimed. The good old days can be today. So Christ says to the Ephesians, "Repent." Literally that means "to change." It must be a change that is maintained, so that we begin and continue to move in a new direction.

How do we change? Put Christ back in the center of our lives. It is an act of our will. It requires consciously placing Him at the core. It means restoring Him to His rightful place as the ultimate priority in our lives—so that everything we do, think, speak, and feel comes from our personal relationship to Christ. We must measure every action by Him; take every signal for behavior from Him; serve because we love Him; witness to please Him; resist sin because it offends Him.

Essential to repentance is maintenance. Repentance is not momentary. It is a sustained change of direction in life. It will require regularly taking time to enhance our relationship with Him at the core. It will mean practicing His presence. It will mean being still and letting Him talk to us. Meet Him in the Word, commune with Him, and the intimacy will grow. The passion will be back in place.

Eventually, after recognizing the need for renewing their relationship, Pat and Jill Williams were able to bring their marriage back to life. My wife, Martie, and I find that we need to get away periodically to renew ourselves and our relationship apart from the fast track of ministry life. It helps to keep our love for each other fresh. Our relationship with the Lord has the same requirements. Take the time to get alone with Him. Fall in love with Him again.

The Greeks had a race in their Olympic games that was unique. The winner was not the runner who finished first. It was the runner who finished with his *torch still lit.* I want to run all the way with the flame of my torch still lit for Him.

The hymnwriter's prayer is mine.

> O, to grace how great a debtor
> Daily I'm constrained to be!
> Let Thy goodness, like a fetter,
> Bind my wandering heart to Thee:
> Prone to wander, Lord, I feel it,
> Prone to leave the God I love;
> Here's my heart,
> O, take and seal it;
> Seal it for Thy courts above.
>
> (Robert Robinson)

ANTICIPATION

Putting Christ at the core of our lives is not just a mystical, ethereal exercise. It is a choice, a step that will make a difference. What can we expect with Christ at the core? Surrendering to Christ will produce a life that will stand regardless of the environment, a righteousness that will be unique and powerful in an unrighteous world.

3

Life-style:
Living It Out

My first pastorate was in a church-planting ministry in which we moved from a school cafeteria to a school gym to our new property and building. I was so excited as the building was being built that I would go every day to see what progress had been made.

I will never forget the day the twenty foot-wall to the worship center was erected. What a thrill to see that wall rising out of the foundation. Later that day I was banking where the church got its loan. I happened to see the vice president who had helped us put the loan package together. I asked if he had seen the progress of the construction. He said, "Yes, but I'm concerned about that wall. If we get a high wind it will never stand." He then counseled me to notify the construction manager to fortify it with external supports until further construction was done. I did.

The next day the wall was supported by large wooden braces. It was an impressive wall, but it had no intrinsic strength.

STANDING STRONG

God calls us and equips us to be free-standing walls for Him, to be able to withstand the winds and tests of temptation without external support.

I have always been intrigued by the story of Joseph (Genesis 39). When all his support systems were gone—his home, parents, friends, and seemingly even His God—he withstood the seductive advancements of Potiphar's wife. And he did so day after day. He was a free standing moral agent; his righteousness was from the inside out.

I have a friend who is often on the road. He once checked into a motel and soon after he got to his room he heard a knock at the door. He opened it to see a pretty woman standing there who said, "How about some fun tonight?"

What a temptation. Who would know?

But he shut the door on her. He was a free-standing wall of righteousness when there were no supports.

The true test of our righteousness is what we are like when no one is watching, when no one will ever find out.

INSIDE-OUT RIGHTEOUSNESS

Why all this talk about righteousness?

Because a heart for God will produce righteousness in our lives. Life-style without heartstyle before God is no style at all, but genuine heartstyle will produce a righteous life-style. If I have opted for authentic Christianity it will generate righteousness. He wishes to reproduce Himself in me. From the center of my life he stimulates me to righteousness.

It is a matter of living out my first love for Him in a non-righteous world. Being righteous from the inside out is a great challenge today, a greater challenge than ever before for American Christians. The task is more intense because our world is so different.

OUR CHANGING WORLD

Slowly, yet certainly, the world around us has changed.

"The Honeymooners," Jackie Gleason and his gang, played the late-hour rerun circuit here in Detroit a few years ago.

Martie and I enjoyed every minute of the half-hour situation comedy. Though the plots were different, the theme was always the same. In the first few minutes Ralph and Alice would usually have a major domestic confrontation. The program would then follow all the colorful dynamics of the conflict, usually complicated by well-meaning friends like Ralph's buddy Norton. But in the closing minutes, Ralph's determination to make life work would become evident as he threw his arms open to Alice and said, in essence, "Life sure is tough, Alice, but you're still the greatest. We're gonna make it!"

Decades ago "The Honeymooners" reflected the heart of America. It was what we believed. Marriage was for keeps, in good times as well as bad.

Today, prime time has been captured by programs like "Dallas" and "Dynasty," where, if you don't like your partner, you divorce him—or, better yet, shoot him. In those programs unfaithfulness is the name of the game.

Fantasies of material gain and self-indulgence are actualized in our living rooms night after night. And if that is not enough, we entertain ourselves with media violence. The Romans were barbaric; they filled coliseums to watch fellow humans shredded by lions. In our world of advanced technology we can wire violence and destruction right into our living rooms and entertain ourselves with it evening after evening.

We live in a different day.

Since 1973 we have killed 18 million unborn babies without bothering our culture's conscience. Life has become cheap. Our values have been redefined.

If a child is born handicapped, parents can instruct doctors to withhold food from the infant—with court support. The child starves to death in the hospital nursery. It takes about six days.

Homosexuals gain custody of children through foster-care or adoption or, in the case of lesbians, through artificial insemination and rear their children in homes that promote homosexuality.

Everything is open for discussion and consideration in the

arena of public education. Homosexual preferences, atheism, marxism, evolution, and secular humanism are all legitimate territory for our academic inquiry. Everything is acceptable but God, creation, and prayer.

More than 50 percent of our young people live together before they get married.

Pornography is readily available in local drug stores, through video shops, and on cable systems.

More children spend their preschool years with a babysitter or in a day care center than with a mother at home.

Only 15 percent of American families reflect the traditional family model of working father, a mother at home, and at least one child.

Our heroes are different today. In my generation heroes were athletes. Today they are musicians. Check out the buttons and T-shirts. Grotesque and demonic images claim the admiration of our youth. Musicians who look sub-normal and who encourage illicit sex, drugs, rebellion, and suicide fill concert halls across the country. Even some of our athletes present such images.

Some men act like women. Some women want to be like men.

E. V. Hill, the famous black pastor from Los Angeles, captured this trend when he said, "We used to have working men and pretty women. We now have working women and pretty men."

Foundations Destroyed

It is easy to identify with the psalmist who wrote, "The wicked bend their bows; they set their arrows against the strings to shoot from the shadows at the upright in heart. When the foundations are being destroyed, what can the righteous do?" (Psalm 11:2-3). But the psalmist affirms that the righteous do not flee. Rather, they take refuge in the Lord (v. 1) and are reminded that He is still a God of holiness and that He still sovereignly reigns (v. 4). The psalmist is reminded that God is not blinded to the evil but that "He observes the sons of men" (v. 4), and for the wicked there will be judgment (vv. 5-6). He concludes with the clear reminder that "The Lord is righteous, he loves justice; upright men will see his face" (v. 7).

What has happened to our foundations? How did we get to where we are? Why is authentic, inside-out righteousness under such stress? The answer lies in a look through the rear-view mirror to see from whence we have come.

Since its beginning, the behavioral rules of American society have been built on what is called the Judeo-Christian ethic. Simply put, that means that our laws, values, perceptions and decisions were shaped by God's moral code as articulated by Moses and Christ. Before the shift, Americans basically agreed on standards of conduct and life-style. Divorce was frowned on, homosexuality was out, intimacy before marriage was immoral, and adultery was wrong; family was important and motherhood was esteemed. It is not that people were necessarily better. People were just as sinful then as now. But sin was practiced behind closed doors and was not publicly condoned. Pastors could proclaim truth, and the cultural values supported their messages. Parents could teach their children truth, and the schools and society reinforced the teaching. Employers could demand righteous behavior and be upheld by courts and community alike.

That day is gone. What happened? In the fifties and early sixties our philosophers began to teach us that there were no absolutes—no right, no wrong. Everything was relative. An action *might* be right or it *might* be wrong depending on the situation. Joseph Fletcher popularized "situation ethics," and absolutes were out the window. We ran with our new freedoms. "If it feels good, do it" became our slogan of life. All the sin that existed so quietly came out of the closet and was paraded unashamedly, with cultural support. Life was redefined; personal rights became paramount, and self-centered living came into vogue. The pursuit of personal pleasure had few restraints.

We then began to notice the fruit of the change. Campus dorms became open for friends of the opposite sex. Child discipline was old-fashioned. Bible reading and prayer in school was forbidden by our laws. The murder of innocent, unborn children as a birth control measure was condoned by our Supreme Court. The women's movement reduced motherhood and homemaking to a second class slot in our culture. Drugs found their way into nearly every schoolyard and college campus. Pornography became more explicit and more readily available. Family was redefined to mean any two people living together— in some states "he-he" or "she-she" marriages constituted families. Politicians began to court gay rights groups. The women's movement became characterized as an anti-family, pro-lesbian force as liberationists burned their bras in the public squares. Sex was "liberated" through the new morality. Music became the god of the young, and Satanic rock groups filled coliseums as they drove the message home with pornographic lyrics that depicted rebellion, violence, death, drugs, illicit sex, and suicide. Authority was wrested in the individual. Personal preferences ruled. Homosexuality came out of the closet and demanded a legitimate place in society. Television accelerated the change through sitcoms that laughingly put down the old values and elevated the new. Magazines, novels, newspapers and syndicated columns all proclaimed the good news that we were finally free from the old rules.

NEW RULES

With the passing of the Judeo-Christian ethic a whole new list of beliefs came to the fore. They are now the rules by which America lives.

Narcissism. In classical literature there is a story about a man named Narcissus, who looked in a pond, saw his reflection, and fell in love with himself. Sociologists have called the seventies the "Me Generation." We learned to live for ourselves. Phrases like "Look out for number one," "Stick up for your rights," "self-actualization," and "self-fulfillment" became standards of behavior. The process of decision-making started with "what is best for me?"

Pluralism. With the passing of absolutes came the acceptance of all systems of thought as basically legitimate. Nothing was invalid. There really was no ultimate truth. Hinduism is OK if it works for you; Marxism is of value. Christianity is fine but not final. If it works for you it's great, but do not impose it as the only way. There are many "true" systems of thought.

Hedonism. The pursuit of pleasure as the meaning of existence came to the fore with the emergence of the Playboy empire. The issue of life now became my personal happiness and pleasure, not what is right or wrong. A man who was wrestling with a sinful habit once told me that he was not sure he wanted to stop sinning because he enjoyed it so much. A *Newsweek* cover article on abortion concluded that the central issue at the core of a decision to terminate the life of an unborn child was the health and/or the *happiness* of the mother.

Secularism. Our culture now makes a clear distinction between the sacred and the secular. Sacred things belong in church on Sundays or in peoples' hearts. The rest of the world is secular, and the two should never mix. Therefore, prayer and the discussion of or the contemplation of God are no longer a welcome part of our society.

Materialism. What counts in a person's life? What he owns, where he lives, his clothes, his club, his cars, boats, and toys are the symbols of success and prestige. We live to gain. Accumulation has become the national anthem of the modern American way.

Relativism. There are no absolutes. Everything is relative. Therefore, everyone is his own authority over every issue in his own life. Whatever works, feels good, or satisfies his longing is OK. All the old, authoritative rules are gone.

Those are the new rules in a society set adrift from its moorings. They each contradict the kingdom values of Christ. They are counter-positioned to righteousness. As a result, they generate unrighteousness. they describe the kind of world in which we seek to generate Christ-at-the-core, inside-out righteousness. The new rules are the gusts that will blow against and test the strength of our free-standing wall.

As free-standing walls, we must seek the righteousness of servanthood—righteousness that affirms that truth is revealed in God's Word and that it is not pluralistic; righteousness that comes from a life that is bent on pleasing God instead of fulfilling personal desires; righteousness that is produced from viewing all of life as a sacred encounter; from viewing material things as a means to advance Christ's kingdom; from seeing right and wrong as absolute; and from placing ourselves under the authority of the Word of God.

Who Has Changed?

Rip Van Winkle slept, and the world changed. But he woke up to find that he had changed as well. We may very well be the Rip Van Winkles of our generation.

Our world has changed, but in the process, more tragically, believers in Christ have changed. We have lost the edge of righteousness—that very thing that makes us both different and effective.

Our sensitivity to authority has changed. By and large we Christians pick and choose what we like to hear and like to believe, what we like to do and not do. The absolute authority of God's Word is often lost in the shuffle of our personal preferences.

Our sense of purity has changed. Things on television that once caused red flags in our spirits may even bring a smile to our faces. There was a time when Christians did not go to movies. Many now go indiscriminately and freely talk about what they have seen. We subscribe to channels on our cable systems that bring unrighteousness into our living rooms. I hear us saying that we are "mature enough" to handle the input of nudity, pornographic innuendo, and violence. The movies we used to boycott were like Sunday school picnics compared to what we now watch at home and pay to see in our theaters.

We preach less of heaven, hell, and eternity and more of this life, happiness, and temporal success.

We are becoming more comfortable with the use of alcohol as a beverage—while the world becomes more concerned about its effects.

Our churches refuse to deal with the breakup of the home, immorality, and divisive behavior among their members.

Success by the world's standards has become the goal of churches that go to any lengths to become big and well-known. Instead of complementing one another, our churches compete to be the "largest" or "fastest growing" in our communities.

Materialism and the pursuit of pleasure, health, and happiness are now proclaimed by television evangelists and pastors alike as being the highest achievement of a person's faith.

We have lulled ourselves with our liturgy while ignoring the desperate plight of a hurting world in which brokenness and poverty of spirit are rampant (see Isaiah 58).

Institutions of learning once used of God to train godly people to minister with zeal and commitment in the church and community now downplay personal sanctification and retain faculty that produce skepticism and doubt in student's hearts.

Seminaries that were founded to teach sound doctrine and prepare men for ministry openly deny the inerrancy of Scripture and cast doubts on the historicity of God's Word yet continue to have a measure of respectability in evangelical circles.

Some have awakened but have recoiled into a legalistic isolationism that was unknown to our fathers. Such isolationism leaves us unable to influence our world for Christ.

We are losing. Losing the indispensable edge of our uniqueness in Christ. Holiness, purity, righteousness, and justice have been lost in a subliminal capitulation to an alien system of thoughts, values, and orders of behavior. We find ourselves conformed to the image of this world (Romans 12:2).

We must hear God's call to be conformed afresh to Christ (Romans 8:28), to reestablish biblical principles that will give rise to non-negotiable biblical convictions—convictions that will produce the righteousness of an indwelling Christ, convictions that are actualized because Christ is at the core.

If we do not reestablish personal righteousness in our changing world, we will forfeit our ability to make a difference in people's lives. Impact on our world demands the uniqueness of Christ. We cannot make a difference if we are not different. We will lose our next generation.

We will lose our good report before God as we ultimately stand before him bereft of gold, silver, and precious stones. We will be nothing more than ash-heap Christians in the charred remains of our wood, hay, and stubble (1 Corinthians 3:12).

The stakes are high.

A Place to Start: Discernment

Is it possible to live righteously in a secularized world that is now diametrically opposed to biblical values? How do we live righteously in a world that has redefined our sexuality, loyalties, desires, and appetites? How can we be counter-cultural and maintain our distinctiveness? How can we not be seduced and reduced by the bombardment of this pagan secularism? How can we be uniquely Christian as singles, young people, couples, parents, corporate leaders, and senior citizens?

It begins with discernment. Discernment in Scripture is the skill that enables us to differentiate. It is the ability to see issues clearly. We desperately need to cultivate this spiritual skill that will enable us to know right from wrong. We must be prepared to distinguish light from darkness, truth from error, best from better, righteousness from unrighteousness, purity from defilement, and principles from pragmatics.

The writer of Hebrews states that our goal as Christians

should be the ability to discern the things that are good from the things that are evil.

> We have much to say about this, but it is hard to explain because you are slow to learn. In fact, though by this time you ought to be teachers, you need someone to teach you the elementary truths of God's word all over again. You need milk, not solid food! Anyone who lives on milk, being still an infant, is not acquainted with the teaching about righteousness. But solid food is for the mature, who by constant use have trained themselves to distinguish good from evil. (Hebrews 5:11-14)

The text delineates five key elements of discernment.

First, discernment demands that we must be *ready to learn* what is taught about righteousness (vv. 11-13). The writer indicts his readers for being slow learners—literally, unwilling to hear. When I was a child I would often stick my fingers in my ears if I did not like what was being said. I sense that people do that in my congregation from time to time. We have pre-decided what we want to be and what we want to do. If the Word makes us uncomfortable, we are prone to reject the input. It is discounted and discarded and we remain as unrighteous infants. God's Word may make us uncomfortable. It will place us in tension. But that tension is always the beginning of growth and maturity.

The cause of the tension will be God's "teaching about righteousness" (v. 3). It is our responsibility to hear and incorporate God's teaching on righteousness whether it is comfortable or not. That teaching about righteousness then becomes our measuring stick for right and wrong.

Second, the text states that our *discernment is a mark of our maturity*. Our maturity is not in our years of being saved, our position in the church, our wealth, our health, or even our knowledge of theology or the Scriptures (Hebrews 6:1-2). The demonstration of maturity is in the skill of distinguishing clearly between what is right or wrong.

Third, it is clear that *righteousness is the goal of discernment* (vv. 13-14). Every thought, choice, action, and reaction must be formed by what we know from God's Word about right and wrong, good and evil. A desire to be discerning comes from a desire to produce righteousness, which drives us to search for the principle of righteousness so that we might establish ourselves in righteousness.

Fourth, *discernment is our personal responsibility.* Note the emphasis in the personal pronouns: "*who* by constant use have trained *themselves.*" We have shortchanged ourselves by imposing righteousness upon each other in forms of external systems. Discernment is a personal, internal skill that equips us to reflect Christ's righteousness by hearing and then using the "word of righteousness" in a variety of situations in our lives.

Fifth, we are to be consistently using the solid food, that is, this teaching about righteousness, that we might *train ourselves in discernment.* Discernment is a skill. It takes practice and perseverance. When a situation of life intercepts us, we are to search the Word for relevant teaching about righteousness. When we discover it, we apply the principle to that life situation. As we do that consistently, we become highly skilled and are able to discern with great accuracy.

Principles That Produce

What does God provide for those of us who desire a heart-style that produces a distinctive life-style? He provides teaching about righteousness, or standards of right and wrong.

In the Old Testament God warned the merchants of Israel not to cheat their customers by weighing out goods with weights that were inaccurate. Interestingly, the Bible uses the word for "righteous" to describe good and fair weights. Righteousness is that which measures accurately to a standard. Even today we have a Bureau of Weights and Measurements.

All our merchandise must meet their established criteria. From peas to prime rib, a pound must be a pound.

In His Word God has given us a set of standards or principles. These are our tools for discernment. They enable us to distinguish between right and wrong. They are principles that we can personally own at the heart level regardless of environmental influences and pressures. By them we can evaluate each perception and decision of life. We embrace these principles because our inner flame for Christ seeks to generate a righteousness consistent to His. They provide the power to produce free-standing walls of righteousness in the face of unrighteousness.

A biblical principle is a rule that has a multiplicity of applications. Christ, in His encounter with the Pharisees concerning rules of righteousness, made a remarkable statement. He taught that righteousness begins with two foundational principles: Love God; love others. Those two commands can be applied in many ways. In fact, after articulating the two commands Christ made a phenomenal claim. He said, *"All the law . . . hang on these two commandments"* (Matthew 22:34-40, italics added). Slicing through a complex, unrighteous world are two simple yet profound commitments, commitments that begin with our relationship to God and spill out into our relations with others in all kinds of settings. Although the New Testament expands on each of these rules, they remain the centerpoint of God's system of authentic and effective righteousness.

These rules provide a "grid," a set of decision-making standards with which we make our choices. They provide a foundation for discernment. For example, when shopping I ask myself several questions before making a purchase. Do I need it? Can I afford it? Can I use it to glorify God? Could I use the money in a more constructive way? Will it be of benefit to my effectiveness for Christ? What kind of impact will it have on our family?

There are at least six principles, all growing out of our love for God and others, that provide a biblical grid through which we run every decision. It is a grid that will produce a genuine righteousness. These six principles will be developed in the ensuing chapters. However, we must first clearly understand the character of authentic righteousness in contrast to the false and dangerous righteousness of the pharisees.

4

Rules in Perspective: Code or Principles

When Christ gave the commands to love God and to love others, He presented a classic confrontation between two systems of behavior—Christ's system and the system of the Pharisees. Their system was externally imposed; His was internal. Theirs was complex; His was concise. Theirs was burdensome; His was liberating. The system of the Pharisees produced a false, proud, and divisive form of righteousness; His produced true godliness.

In Matthew 22:34-40 the Pharisees come to Christ and ask, "Teacher, which is the greatest commandment in the Law?" For them it was a significant question, because they lived under a religious system that contained 613 specific laws. That is exactly why they needed religious lawyers, "experts in the law" (v. 35) Such spiritual attorneys worked full time at knowing, interpreting, and issuing official rulings about their laws of righteousness. In the face of that system Christ announced simply and concisely that there were really only two laws: to love God and to love your neighbor. The contrast is vivid.

CODE ETHICS

Christ and the Pharisees shared a desire for standards of

righteousness, but that is about all they had in common. In contrast to the two commands of Christ, the Pharisees had developed a system of 613 laws, 365 negative commands and 248 positive laws. That complex system was an *external* code of specific rules imposed by the religious establishment *upon* the people. It was burdensome and demanding. That external system of codes was presented to Christ so that He might pick which of the 613 was the most important.

THE CODE ETHICS OF THE PHARISEES

For lack of a better term we will call such a system *code ethics* because it provides an extensive list of codes that detail behavior patterns for specific situations of life. The Pharisees developed their code system over many generations. By the time Christ came it had produced a heartless, cold, and arrogant brand of righteousness. As such, it contained at least ten tragic flaws.

(1) The first flaw is that *new laws continually need to be invented for new situations.* That is how God's original few became 613. When a new situation arose, a new law was written. They soon became confusing and complex.

(2) Since new laws are needed for new situations, people tend to look to those in a place of spiritual authority to articulate the new rules. Those under the rules then feel spiritually accountable to these spiritual leaders for compliance to the rules. Hence *accountability to God is replaced by accountability to men.* That is why those caught up in this dynamic often fall when they are away from human points of accountability.

(3) Code ethics *reduces a person's ability to personally discern* the difference between right and wrong. Specific righteousness is already defined, and the rules are taught to them by others. They never have "trained themselves to distinguish good from evil" (Hebrews 5:14).

(4) Code ethics creates a *judgmental spirit*. The Pharisees were constantly measuring others by their own man-made system of righteousness. If you did not measure up you were ostracized. Even Christ was judged by their system and was found wanting.

(5) The Pharisees *confused personal preferences with divine law*. In their system they had created what they called "fence laws," designed to help keep themselves clear of breaking the divine law. For example, God had commanded them not to commit adultery; a fence law may have commanded not to touch a woman. Their desire for spiritual safety soon took on equal weight with revealed divine law. The resulting rules were then imposed on others, and in time they were given greater weight than divine law. Those are the "traditions" that Christ spoke against on so many occasions.

(6) Code ethics *produces inconsistencies*. Laws created for one particular situation became a problem in another situation. So in order to handle the new situation, a new law would be made that produced a striking contradiction to the old law. One of their "fence laws" to protect the Sabbath was that husking grain on the Sabbath was wrong because it was "labor." A case was later brought to the Pharisees in which a man had laid a spoon, sticky with honey, on an ear of grain. When he lifted the spoon the husk came off. Had he been guilty of breaking the Sabbath? They decided in that case it was not a breach of the law. From that point on, Jews were able to husk their grain on the Sabbath with sticky spoons. Their behavior became inconsistent and hypocritical.

(7) The code system of behavior also created a *false standard of righteousness*. Righteousness was measured on the basis of whether or not you followed their rules rather than on a heart-level relationship to God. In fact, because the system was externally imposed and externally policed, a person really

had no need for a growing relationship to God. It was just a matter of pleasing the standards of the system. That is why Christ reproved them for being whitewashed gravestones. They had ritual with no relationship.

(8) The Pharisaical system of rules *became a burden* to the Jews. Who could ever master a set of 613 rules? You would need a little red wagon to pull the volumes of laws and their interpretations around just to stay on top of everything. The system inhibited, intimidated, and enslaved God's people. It placed them in servitude to the proud, Pharisaical leadership. That is the system Christ sought to break, and that is why he told the Jews that if they knew the truth the truth would set them free.

(9) Code ethics were *strictly external.* The emphasis of the system was not on character but rather on behavior. Christ told the Pharisees that they were greedy, dishonest, and proud, wanting simply to please men. That is a strong indictment to a group that behaved so well. William Coleman in his book *A Pharisee's Guide to Total Holiness* states that Pharisees were ultimately concerned with only one thing: "How do I look?" They needed to be reminded that man looks on the outward appearance, but God looks on the heart (1 Samuel 16:7).

(10) Finally, code ethics were *rejected by Christ.* We tend to think that strictness is next to godliness. The Pharisees sincerely thought they were pleasing God. They could not have been more strict, yet Christ demonstrated that they were more strict than God. There are many cults and sects today that are more strict than the strictest of Christians. God is not pleased with those cults. The Pharisees had put requirements on people that God never intended, which is exactly why Christ had to remind them that the Sabbath was made for man and not man for the Sabbath (Mark 2:27). Whereas most of us are con-

cerned about becoming too lax in our life-style, code ethics failed by creating traditions that were too strict. We should remember that ungodliness is any deviation from God's standard, whether it be to the right or to the left.

CODE ETHICS TODAY

We must be aware that there is a great danger of being caught up in code ethics today. There is a subtle, ever-present tendency to move from principles to codes. As we apply God's principles it is easy for the applications to form new rules that come to be regarded as divine law. Our preferences quickly become confused with the convictions that are based on divine revelation and soon take on the weight of divine law. Those cultural or personal preferences may in time become irrelevant, and if the application has become a rule we have false and irrelevant standards of righteousness. In the sixties many Christians, in an effort not to be identified with the rebellion, illicit sexuality, and the substance abuse of the hippies, refused longer hair and shaved their beards. In some cases they even specified that a man's hair should not touch his ears or the collar of his shirt. That was not a bad application of the principle to "be wise in the way you act toward outsiders" (Colossians 4:4). Some, however, made the application a divine rule. And now, when the application is no longer relevant, some still maintain it as a rule and standard of spirituality. In such ways we become burdened with non-biblical baggage and create a spirit of judgment, division, and false spirituality within the Body.

I know of churches that refuse to let their soloists hold the microphones in their hands when they sing. To them it represents a worldly approach to music. Unfortunately they claim it as their biblical conviction. Their preference, to which they are entitled, has been elevated to the level of divine revelation; those who agree are spiritual, and those who do not are less than righteous.

In code ethics today discernment is destroyed. Many who would never attend a movie theater watch worse things at home on their televisions and VCRs with little twinge of conscience. Code ethics has made the theater the issue, whereas the real issues are personal purity, choosing what is excellent, the protection of the mind, and separation from influences that defeat us spiritually. Because the code says do not go to the movies the wrong issue is raised, and discernment is lost.

Our modern system of code ethics focuses its adherents on the system and on those who dictate and enforce it. Therefore, as soon as people are away from the influence of the code and out of sight from the "enforcers," they are prone to the seduction of many opportunities to sin.

As it was with the Pharisees, a code ethic becomes burdensome and often causes a tragic backlash in ensuing generations. It generates a stagnate and stale brand of Christian experience. It produces arrogance and hollowness at the core. It tends to lock people into spiritual infancy. It stifles authentic Christianity. Alexander Solzhenitsyn writes, "Whenever the issue of life is woven of legalistic relationships, this creates an atmosphere of spiritual mediocrity that paralyzes man's noblest impulses."

To protect ourselves from code ethics there are several questions we can ask.

To whom do I feel accountable for my behavior?

Am I able to personally discern issues of right and wrong, not based on how I feel or how others may feel but on clear principles from God's Word?

Do I tend to judge the spirituality of others by my own preferences?

Do I feel "spiritual" because of what I do and do not do?

Am I able to clearly differentiate between personal, cultural preferences and the clear convictions that are divinely revealed?

Is my system of righteousness a burdensome ritual, or is it a genuine expression of my first love for Christ?

If code ethics was rejected by Christ, then what kind of standards are there by which righteousness is measured? The standards are the principles of God's Word. God's principles are *basic commands* that have a multiplicity of application. It is important to see clearly the function of a principle in contrast to a code.

Though Christ's system of principle righteousness was diametrically opposed to code ethics, there is one thing He and the Pharisees did have in common. Both systems affirm the importance of commands (Matthew 22:36, 38, 40). It is important to hear Christ affirm for us the necessity of commands because in many corners of the kingdom "rules" have fallen on hard times. Those hard times have come for at least three reasons.

OUR PROBLEM WITH GOD'S RULES

(1) We have an *authority crisis* in the church. It is a spillover from our culture. Our humanistic culture has, in essence, said that men are gods, able to determine and dictate their own existence. Hence, we are encouraged to sovereignly rule in the sphere of our own affairs.

A couple once stood in my office faced with a choice. The Bible was clear about what they should do. They left, openly admitting that they would do just the opposite. There was no remorse or shame. They simply did not agree with what God's Word had to say.

I have been in groups discussing issues of righteousness and heard believers say, "Well, it doesn't mean that to me." They have said it about clear biblical statements of righteousness. They are saying in essence that they will interpret Scripture to fit their own desires.

Or we say, "That may be what it says, but I just can't do that." Or, "I know that's what the Bible says, but I've always been this way and I'll never change." Some who are more transparent say, "I don't care what it says; this is what I want to do."

In whatever form it is stated, we basically say that the only rules in life are my rules and that only if God's rules happen to agree with my preferences will I submit.

(2) Also working against God's "rules" is the *backlash against legalism*. There has been a great swing of the pendulum away from externally imposed codes, and in the process we have become libertines. Those who have biblical convictions are branded as legalists, and Christian liberty is construed as the permission for everyone to do as he sees fit. It was to this tendency that Paul wrote, "Do not use your freedom to indulge the sinful nature" (Galatians 5:13).

(3) Finally, *our view of grace* can even dull the edge of God's commands. Because God's grace has covered all my unrighteousness, sin does not seem detrimental. As we are about to sin we remind ourselves that all we have to do is claim 1 John 1:9. We should remember that God's Word also teaches, "Do not be deceived; God cannot be mocked. A man reaps what he sows. The one who sows to please his sinful nature, from that nature will reap destruction" (Galatians 6:7-8). As Paul said, "Shall we go on sinning that grace may increase? By no means!" (Romans 6:1-2). The writer of the book to the Hebrews had some hard words for those who insult the spirit of grace (Hebrews 10).

THE PURPOSE OF GOD'S COMMANDS

It is important to remind ourselves that rules of righteousness are important to God. He underscores them in both the Old and New Testaments. The New Testament did not cancel God's rules; it reaffirmed and at times intensified the commands. All the Decalogue was reinstituted by Christ except for the Sabbath. To discount God's laws is to misunderstand what they are.

God's commands are first of all a reflection of God's righteousness in human terms. Some of us seem to think that at one point in eternity past God contemplated what He could do to make life difficult for us and came up with the Ten Commandments. The commandments are not arbitrary rules from a careless divine being. Romans 3:21 indicates that they are actually the revelation of God's righteousness in human terms. They reflect what it means to be like God in the sphere of our existence. We are not to commit adultery because God is a faithful God and is loyal to His covenants and promises. Lying is wrong because God is a God of truth and cannot lie. If He were here he would not covet because He is a self-contained entity and needs nothing; hence we should not covet because He is always with us ready to supply all our needs (Philippians 4:19, Hebrews 13:5-6). God is righteous. As such He is our standard for righteousness. His commands communicate the standards of His character and therefore serve as the righteous standards for our lives.

God's commands are also given for our personal safety and prosperity (Deuteronomy 5:33, 1 John 5:3). Because God has created us and our world, He knows what will and will not be profitable for us. His commands keep us on track. They keep us out of trouble. They keep us safe.

The tremendous outbreak of social diseases is a clear illustration of that truth. God knew that sexual promiscuity, unfaithfulness, and homosexuality would cause severe medical problems. He knew that our chemical makeup would not cope with that perversion of His creation, so he gave His laws to protect us. The answer to the epidemics of VD, herpes, and AIDS is to submit to His laws. They are meant for our prosperity.

When my eldest son was quite small, his older friends played ball in the street. When he would ask to play ball in the street I would tell him no. I did not mind if he played ball. He just could not play in the street. Why? There was danger there that he would not be able to cope with. I loved him and did not want his body integrated into the grill of a Mack truck. God knows where Satan's traffic is. He loves us enough to warn and redirect us. He does it through His commands.

God's rules also help us know God's expectations for us, so that we can know how to please Him in our life-style. When David briefed Solomon about being the next king he told his son, "Observe what the Lord your God requires . . . keep his decrees and commands, his laws and requirements . . . so that you may prosper in all you do and wherever you go" (1 Kings 2:2-3).

A father once sat in my office lamenting his teenage daughter's behavior. I asked him if he had clearly delineated what he expected of her. To my surprise he said, "No." How was she to know what he expected? I am thankful that God has clearly prescribed His requirements for me. There is a special security in knowing how to please Him.

Actually, we should be grateful for God's rules. They enable us to understand what God expects; they keep us safe, and they chart a course for God's kind of righteousness through us in this world. It is no wonder that David wrote,

> Blessed is the man who does not walk in the counsel of the wicked or stand in the way of sinners or sit in the seat of mockers. But his delight is in the law of the Lord, and on his law he meditates day and night. He is like a tree planted by streams of water, which yields its fruit in season and whose leaf does not wither. Whatever he does prospers. (Psalm 1:1-3)

We should exclaim with him, "Oh, how I love your law! I meditate on it all day long" (Psalm 119:97).

WHERE DO WE BEGIN

God's first law of righteousness, the priority principle, is to love the Lord your God with all our heart, soul, and mind (Matthew 22:37). It is significant that the first standard of righteousness is framed within the context of my relationship with

Him. It is also significant that it is to be from the heart, soul, and mind. That is a requirement that begins with heartstyle and flows from my relationship with Him at the core.

What does it mean to love God? In what way does that principle liberate us to produce righteousness from the inside out? In the next three chapters the issue of loving God will be pursued in three dimensions.

5

Loving God:
The Principle of Surrender

A seminary student recently asked me, "What does it really mean to love God?" He had grown up in a strong Christian environment. He had attended a Christian college and was now in graduate work heading for Christian ministry. His question was significant because he had come this far in his Christian experience without a solid definition of Christianity's most important component. His numbers are legion among believers today. Those who can recite a clipped catechismal definition are often wanting in both understanding and application. All of us must ask his question if we are genuinely interested in righteousness. Christ said it was the priority standard by which we discern right and wrong.

There is nothing more important in living out our first love for Christ than our appreciation for and application of this primary principle of righteousness. Sadly, for many of us loving God does not play at center stage. It is at best an idea that is often spoken but not inbred. For those who have opted to live by code ethics it has never been important to know what it means. A code system operates well without it. If we have let Christ slip from the core, if we have lapsed into ritual and devotionless duty, loving God is a non-issue.

But if we are committed to ignite the flame of our hearts by putting Christ at the core, and if we have chosen now to internally produce righteousness through personally-owned principles of Scripture, then loving God is the indispensable, non-negotiable place to start.

Indispensable, Non-Negotiable

How significant is it? Christ said that loving God is the "first and greatest commandment" (Matthew 22:38). Three words underscore its importance. "First" and "greatest" tell us that loving God is indispensable; "commandment" describes it as a non-negotiable part of our ethical repertoire.

I possess many dispensable items. I could live without a car, a house, a friend, a family—even without a hand or a leg. But I cannot live without my heart. That is indispensable to my existence. It is that central reality from which all of life flows. The Greek word translated "first" means that thing to which everything else is subsequent, consequent, dependent, or secondary. The word translated "greatest" means more important in rank or position. Loving God is the centerpoint, the starting point, and the ultimate priority; nothing is more essential to the life of righteousness.

Not only is loving God indispensable, but it is also non-negotiable. Christ's commands are absolute statements to which we conform. They are expressions of His righteousness in human terms—the standards by which we prosper and the requirements for pleasing Him. Christian ethics are not governed by committee or majority vote. Biblical righteousness does not begin with our preferences. God's righteousness is settled and authoritative. God does not change His standards to conform to us. His standards are the expression of what is right, and our behavior becomes righteous as we come into alignment with them.

The Response

Knowing how to love is important to good relationships. Any man who is committed to a growing friendship knows how to express his love to his sweetheart. It means flowers, little surprises, sweet notes, a wink across a crowded room, a mid-morning phone call, a listening ear, and a word of encouragement.

Love is the central expression, the most precious thing we give in a relationship. We give it to our friends, our marriage partners, our children, our cats, and our dogs. It is important to know whether or not we love God. And we must ask, "How do I love God?"

Loving God starts by understanding the profound truth that God has loved us. Not only is it true that He *is* love; it also is true that He *does* love and that He actually has extended His love to us personally in a multitude of ways, primarily expressed in Jesus Christ. He has proved His love in what He has done for us and what He has given to us.

Love generates a response. God's Word states that "we love because He first loved us" (1 John 4:19). God has been the initiator; He simply asks us to respond. Responding is the easiest part of a relationship. Love comes quite naturally and spontaneously when we are loved.

Early in our ministry, our mode of transportation was marginal to say the least. At the close of one a Thanksgiving eve service members of our church, much to our surprise, gave us a set of keys to a new car they had leased for us. I drove away that night with a deep gratefulness toward the flock that had been so sensitive and generous toward us. I had always sought to be faithful in shepherding them, but their love for our family stimulated me to seek new ways to express how much I loved them in return. As nice as the car was, my response was not so much to the car as to the fact that they had said, "We love you, Pastor!" It made it easy to love them back.

The sacrificial, redemptive love of God for us makes our

love for Him a reasonable, well-deserved response. Once we understand the depths of His love, we will desire to express our love for Him in a natural, spontaneous way.

THE ESSENCE

The seminarian's question, "What does it really mean to love God?" deserves a clear and careful answer. It begins with understanding *agapē,* the word that Christ used in Matthew 22:38 for "love." Significantly, *agapē* is not primarily an emotional kind of love; God is not asking us to always feel good about Him. That is important to me because there are days when I do not feel good about anything. Our emotions can be the result of a tough day at the office, health problems, a missed putt, too much Pepsi and pizza before bedtime, a broken relationship, a change in hormones. Even bad dreams create emotional hangovers. We are not able to press a "feel good" button to suddenly feel like we love God or anyone else. How strange it would be for God to command us to do something that we could not do. *Agapē* love is not primarily a feeling; it is a choice. God always directs His commands to our will, not our emotions. We love Him because we choose to love Him regardless of how we feel.

What does the choice to love God entail? *Agapē* love means to give, to yield, to surrender to another. In essence, Christ is saying that the expression of true love for God, the way that we respond to the fact that He surrendered Himself to meet our sin problem, is to yield to Him as God.

When I move onto an expressway here in the Detroit metroplex there is always a triangle-shaped sign that encourages me to "yield." It means to give way to the flow of traffic, to merge with care. In a sense the will of God moves down through the territory of my life like a major highway. It is His eternal plan and program, with a specific place and specific principles for me. He asks that I yield, that I give way to Him and merge my life into His will. It intercepts my life. Loving Him means yielding to Him.

Knowing the way traffic moves on an expressway, there is no way that I am going to try to intercept one without yielding. An eighteen wheeler would annihilate my poor, defenseless car, to say nothing of my body. So I yield. Trying to buck God's traffic yields the devastating results of sin (James 1:13-15). Yielding is not just a loving thing to do, it is a wise thing to do as well.

Admittedly, though, it is not always easy to yield. I am usually in a hurry when I drive. Yielding tends to make me late. Yielding in traffic sometimes means swallowing my pride to let someone go ahead. As we lovingly yield to our Lord we may be asked to yield our preferences, our pride, our passions, our desires, our dreams, our possessions, our time, our resources, and even our friends and family. Yet loving God is the ultimate priority. The significance of yielding is that yielding my will for the sake of His will is the ultimate statement of how much I love Him. He does not want words, ritual, or habits. He wants us to love Him with our hearts and choices. He wants us to prove to Him that He is truly worth more than anything else to us.

As my life merges with His revealed will, I lay the baggage of all my selfish and sinful choices at the base of the Yield sign and then get caught up in the momentum of the flow of His good and perfect will for me.

Yielding to God is not merely what I should do, although it certainly is the right thing to do. Yielding to God is not merely the wise thing to do because it is for my ultimate prosperity. And yielding to God is not merely what we do to produce righteousness from the "inside out" in a terribly unrighteous culture. Yielding to God is the tangible way that we say, "I love you." Love looks for significant ways to prove itself. The significance of the gift is not so much in the gift itself as it is in the thought that it expresses. This is exactly why Andrae Crouch wrote to God,

How can I say thanks for the things you have done for me?

Things so undeserved that you gave to prove your love for me.
The voices of a million angels could not express my gratitude.
All that I am and ever hope to be,
I owe it all to Thee.*

When I think of loving God by yielding to Him, I like to see the concept in terms of the word *surrender.* Romans 6-8 depicts graphically the strength of the flesh as we struggle to yield to God. Yielding often requires a battle. Our passion and pride can be a powerful force to yield. We would often rather love ourselves than the Savior. But surrender is the privileged response of our love. Surrender is our valentine to our Father, Savior, Redeemer, and Friend.

<h3 style="text-align:center">TERMS OF SURRENDER</h3>

There are six dynamics that form the terms of surrender to our God. These dynamics bring the process of surrender into clear focus.

Surrender is *by choice.*

Surrender is *continuous.* The Greek verb indicates a continuous commitment to the principles of righteousness. It calls us to surrender even when it is inconvenient, when it is uncomfortable, and when it is not what we want to do. God wants no "daisy pluckers" in the fields of His kingdom—"I love Him, I love Him not, I love Him, I love Him not . . ."

Surrender is *proper.* Note that we are commanded to love the Lord. The name *Lord* reveals that God holds the rightful place of authority over us. He has a divine right to rule in my life. His proper place as Lord would be sufficient in and of itself to require my surrender.

Surrender is *sweet.* I love the fact that surrender is a positive command that focuses not on duty or activity but rather on my relationship with God. An intimate relationship is always

* "My Tribute," by Andrae Crouch. © Copyright 1971 by Lexicon Music, Inc. International copyright secured. All rights reserved. Used by permission.

more rewarding than duties and activities. In fact, a good relationship provides the energy for good behavior in the relationship.

Our surrender becomes sweet as we note that Matthew 22:37 asks us to love the Lord *our God*. When we think of who we are surrendering to, it becomes a sweet surrender. I can remember one of my first dates with my then future wife, Martie. We were young and in college. It was a beautiful fall morning, and we were walking down a country road. I was wild about her, but I did not know how she felt toward me. As we walked down that road I began to perceive that she liked me. Wow! The vibrations were there. I want you to know that my heart surrendered on the spot. If she had said, "Climb that tree," I would have. How high? When should I come down? How far out on the limb? The relationship had caught fire, and she was worth my surrender. It was a sweet surrender indeed.

The phrase "love the Lord *your God*" speaks to the fact that we belong to Him in a covenant relationship. We have been adopted by Him (Ephesians 1:5). Adoption is more significant than birth because adoption is by choice. I was required to take all three of our children as they were because they were born to us. Boy, girl, big, little, we took what we got. Frankly, I was thrilled with all three, but in reality I was stuck with them. I could not give them back. God, however, was not "stuck" with me. He chose me. He walked into the territory of my life, saw me dirty and rebellious in my sin, and by choice adopted me, became my God, and cut me into the inheritance of the riches of His glory. He selected me to be a child of the King. Ephesians 1:4-8, 13-14 states,

> He chose us in him before the creation of the world to be holy and blameless in his sight. In love he predestined us to be adopted as his sons through Jesus Christ, in accordance with his pleasure and will—to the praise of his glorious grace, which he has freely given us in the One he loves. In him we have redemption through his blood, the forgiveness of sins, in accordance with the riches of God's grace that he

lavished on us with all wisdom and understanding. . . . And you also were included in Christ when you heard the word of truth, the gospel of your salvation. Having believed, you were marked in him with a seal, the promise of the Holy Spirit, who is a deposit guaranteeing our inheritance until the redemption of those who are God's possession—to the praise of his glory.

In light of that, it is a sweet surrender.

Surrender is a *personal* and *internal*. It is a surrender with the *heart, soul, and mind.* No one can impose this surrender on you. It is a personal privilege and a personal responsibility. Refusing to surrender is not rebellion against a parent, pastor, or peer group. It is rebellion against God and God alone. We surrender personally to our God at the level of our inner being. God is not interested in an empty, external relationship.

Surrender is *complete.* The little word "all" consumes the entirety of what we are. We live in a world that negotiates on the basis of percentages. It is hard to believe, but baseball players make hundreds of thousands of dollars a year for hitting the ball one out of three times at bat. We invest our money based on the percentage yield. A 10 to 20 percent yield catches our attention. But with Christ, it is nothing short of 100 percent surrender. He never negotiates on the basis of percentages; every corner of our lives is to be surrendered. There is to be nothing between our soul and the Savior. If we chain off a segment of our existence, He will begin to hack away at the chain. A limited love is really not much love at all.

THE FOCUS OF SURRENDER

Some of us may be saying, "I don't always like to surrender." I understand. I have heard my own stubborn heart say that on occasion. What sobers me, though, is the fact that I surrender every time I make a decision. I surrender to the adversary, or I surrender to the one who loves me and deserves my love in return. The real issue of our love for the Lord is not whether we will surrender but rather to what or to whom we will surrender.

The competition for our surrender is fierce. Our own lusts, desires, and dreams allure us. Our vengeful and defensive responses beckon us to surrender to them. The selfish use of our talents and money, the lure of fame and fortune, comfort and convenience, and acceptance by the world around are all strong forces that threaten to lure us into their temples, asking us to surrender there. We are seduced at every turn of life from within and from without.

The irony is that we are allured to surrendering to sin *by the very gifts that God has given us;* talents, sensuality, money, and intelligence are used by the adversary to lure us away from our Lord. God wants us to surrender all those marvelous gifts to His glory, but if we are not watchful the gift may soon become more valuable to us than the Giver of the gift. That was exactly the point when God Asked Abraham to sacrifice his son Isaac. As Hebrews says, it was a test. A test of Abraham's priority love. Isaac had become very important to Abraham: "your son, your only son, Isaac, whom you love" (Genesis 22:2). Isaac was God's special gift to Abraham. But did Isaac get in the way of Abraham's loving allegiance to God? No. As special as Isaac was, Abraham kept God as the priority point of surrender in his life. He loved his God and so was willing to surrender the gift back to the giver if necessary. We will cease to love Him the day the gifts become of greater worth than He who gives them.

In the midst of heavy temptation Joseph proved he loved God more than the satisfaction of the sensual appetites God had given him. Imagine being seduced day after day by one of Egypt's beautiful women and standing strong when there were no external supports. From whence come men like that? Listen to Joseph's reason for staying out of bed with her: "How then could I do such a wicked thing and sin against God?" (Genesis 39:9). That is solid surrender.

The question for us is the same question that Christ asked

Peter: "Do you truly love me more than these?" (John 21:15). Christ was speaking about the nets Peter had laid on the ground. Discouraged, Peter had left Christ and gone back to his career of fishing. Christ encountered him and drove him back to the ultimate issue: who and what is most important in your life? God is interested in knowing where He places in the league of our living. What we do with our time, money, sensual appetites, friends, family, church involvement, and thought patterns are all expressions of whether or not we love Him.

Why do we reject the onslaught of youthful lusts? Because of Him. We forgive our enemies, submit to the needs of brothers and sisters in Christ, love our wives, submit to our husbands, nurture our children, guard our minds, and pursue holiness and personal purity because of Him.

All of this, not because it has become a list of dos and don'ts, but because my heart is rightly and gladly set in surrender to Him. Such surrender of the heart keeps the fire of righteousness ablaze in my life. My actions and reactions are no longer dependent on circumstances, enforcers, peer pressure, or emotions. I love my wife, not because she deserves it or even because I always feel like it. I love her because my Father wills it, and I am set on surrender to Him. I forgive, regardless of the offense or offender, because my heart is set to love God by surrendering to Him. I use my money as expression of my love for Him and His kingdom work. All I do I do for Him. Nothing else matters. Loving God is the purest and strongest motivation for righteousness.

It makes sense to hear Christ say that surrender to God is the ultimate priority in my relationship to Him. If my heart is set on surrender, then I will do what He bids me to do. This principle has a multiplicity of applications. In fact, it serves as my first question in discerning right from wrong. When faced with a decision in life I must begin by asking, What would it mean to surrender to God at this time? The answers to that question put righteousness into action.

6

Loving God:
The Principle of Templing

They were retarded, both of them, and had been kept for years by an older couple who used them to work on their property. They were housed in a small trailer in the back yard, and when the police arrived they found the stench and filth in the trailer to be almost unbearable. From human waste to rotting food, dirt and bugs—it was a bad, sad place to live.

As I read the account in our paper, I felt a sense of indignation. How degrading to treat anyone the way they had been treated. Had this couple no respect for the value of life, the value of a person? How tragically cruel to provide a place and then permit those people, who really could not help themselves, to live in such danger and disgrace. I knew that I could not, would not live in a place like that, and I looked around the living room and thanked God for a clean and healthy place to live.

I found myself thinking about the fact that as a believer in Christ, I have the profound privilege of hosting and housing my Lord, the Almighty God of Israel. God's Word declares, "Do you not know that your body is a temple of the Holy Spirit, who *is in you,* whom you have received from God? You are not your own; you were bought at a price. Therefore honor God with your body (1 Corinthians 6:19-20, italics added).

As I read that verse I was immediately struck with the fact that a pure and holy God had set up residence in me. I thought of all the clutter and defilement that I force into His residence. I also realized that a genuine, surrendered love for Him would be expressed by providing a temple worthy of His name. Housework is definitely a chore. The old adage "Man may work from sun to sun, but woman's work is never done" is true. It is a matter of staying ahead of the clutter. It means picking up, cleaning, keeping out the dirt, and taking your shoes off at the door! Martie does a great job of keeping our home clean and comfortable. She does it because she loves her family. She does it because she enjoys living in a clean home. She does it because our family's reputation is at stake. In fact, all of us work together to keep our home in shape.

God's Word demands that we respond to the world around us in the context of the reality of His indwelling presence. He calls us to express our love by purifying the temple. As we surrender to this principle we provide for Him a clean place in which to reside and work.

TEMPLING

Throughout the history of mankind God has sought to dwell with His people. That has taken several forms. At first it was fellowship in the garden of Eden. Prior to the actual building of the tabernacle in the wilderness, He would often appear, revealing Himself and His Word to men. After Israel left Egypt, God instructed them to build a portable tabernacle where His presence would dwell. In the land of Canaan God dwelt with them in the Ark of the Covenant, and then under Solomon the Temple was built in Jerusalem. Destroyed by foreign invasion, it was later rebuilt under the leadership of Nehemiah

Then Christ came, was made flesh, and "pitched His tent among us" (John 1:14, literal translation). When Christ was about to leave, He claimed that the time was coming when

God would "temple" *in* us (John 14:15-17). That is the privilege of what both Ezekiel and Jeremiah call the new covenant. Ultimately, God's goal is to establish the new heaven and the new earth where, as Revelation 21:3-5 says,

> And I heard a loud voice from the throne saying, "Now the dwelling of God is with men, and he will live with them. They will be his people, and God himself will be with them and be their God. He will wipe every tear from their eyes. There will be no more death or mourning or crying or pain, for the old order of things has passed away." He who was seated on the throne said, "I am making everything new!" Then he said, "Write this down, for these words are trustworthy and true."

It is clear that one of God's basic desires is to dwell with His own. He dwells with us for several significant reasons. As He encamps on our turf He works through His people and *brings honor to His name* (1 Corinthians 6:19-20). He dwells with us *to help us live successfully* in an unrighteous world. The Holy Spirit is the Comforter, the one who comes alongside to help us know the truth. John 16:13 assures us that "when he, the Spirit of truth, comes, he will guide you into all truth." God also dwells with us to *eliminate the defeat of both covetousness and fear* (Hebrews 13:5-6). He dwells in us *to do a work of conviction in this world* (John 16:7-11). He temples in us *to produce righteousness* through our lives in an unrighteous world (Galatians 5:16-23). He moves into our existence *that He might fellowship and relate to us,* His beloved and redeemed creation (Revelation 3:20). And finally, God dwells with His people *to strengthen us for works of both power and love* (2 Timothy 1:7).

This templing work, then, is purposeful. It is an awesome privilege to be the base of operation for my God. It is also a high privilege that He would desire such an intimate relationship with me. It is a sobering truth that He would choose me and set up residence within me.

TERMS OF TEMPLING

Not only does God's Word inform us of the privileged *purposes* of His dwelling in us, it also speaks to the *responsibilities* that are inherent with His taking up His residency in us. As a seminary student, I worked as a bellman in a luxury hotel in Dallas. The vice president of the United States was coming to the city and chose to stay at the hotel. Everything became different. He reserved an entire floor. Security agents swarmed the hotel to guard him. The whole city knew where he was staying, and it made all of us proud to be working there. I found that I worked a little harder, looked a little sharper, and operated more efficiently. My job had an entirely new focus and atmosphere.

So it is when God dwells in us. His residency makes us sensitive to several important responsibilities.

God is a holy God, perfect, undefiled, flawless, and unsoiled. He is holy in all His works. His holiness demands a particular atmosphere in which to dwell. The fact that He dwells within stimulates us to behave and respond differently.

The tabernacle of the Old Testament provides the most graphic picture of what God's templing requires of us. All the regulations regarding the use and function of the tabernacle were instituted to guard and facilitate the presence of a holy God. The Israelites had to undergo ceremonial cleansings from the defilement of the world in order to come before His presence. There were sacrifices of worship and praise and sacrifices that foreshadowed the sacrifice of Christ to make provision for forgiveness of sin as they came to fellowship and worship with their God. The Old Testament tabernacle had priests who were entrusted with serving the Lord and guarding His holiness. All of the furniture and vessels of service to God in the tabernacle were to be sanctified, set apart and kept clean and undefiled for His use. All those things were required to make a fit place for God to dwell. It is interesting and convicting to note that God ascribes the same terms to His templing within us.

We are called *the temple* or sanctuary of God (1 Corinthians 6:19). We often refer to the place where we meet to worship as "the sanctuary." But God does not dwell in a church building. He dwells in the sphere of my being, and His presence should lead me to a life of personal holiness. Peter writes to believers and says, "As obedient children, do not conform to the evil desires you had when you lived in ignorance. But just as he who called you is holy, so be holy in all you do: for, it is written: 'Be holy because I am holy'" (1 Peter 1:14-15).

Christ graphically demonstrated the need for *continual cleansing* from sin when He washed the disciples' feet. The foot-washing was a symbol of the fact that not only does Christ totally cleanse us at salvation, but He also offers us continued cleansing as a requirement for our fellowship with Him (John 13:5-17). First John 1:9 guarantees that cleansing. Just as the Old Testament saints cleansed themselves at the Temple, so it is our responsibility to regularly cleanse ourselves for fellowship with Him.

The New Testament is full of allusions to *sacrifices*, sacrifices that we perform in the cathedral of our bodies instead of at a temple. The totality of our being is to be presented as "living sacrifices, holy and pleasing to God" (Romans 12:1). We also sacrifice with words of praise from our lips and the sharing of our resources with others. "Through Jesus, therefore, let us continually offer to God a sacrifice of praise—the fruit of lips that confess his name. And do not forget to do good and to share with others, for with such sacrifices God is pleased" (Hebrews 13:15-16). Giving our money to the Lord's work is pictured as a "fragrant offering, an acceptable sacrifice, pleasing to God" (Philippians 4:18). Paul wrote that his serving the believers at Philippi was a sacrifice, a praise offering to Christ (Philippians 2:17). We now, as the temples of God, are required to present sacrifices to Him, not the sacrifice for sin because Christ already accomplished that on the cross, but sacrifices of worship and thanksgiving.

We too are called *priests,* a "royal priesthood" (1 Peter 2:9).

We are to serve God and guard the holiness of His presence.

We too are *vessels* to be sanctified in His presence and for His use. Paul speaks of the parts of our bodies as "instruments" sanctified for the Master's use (Romans 6:13; 1 Thessalonians 4:3-4).

God's terms of templing within us come down to three foundational demands: (1) personal purity—because God dwells in us we are to guard ourselves against the defilement of the world so that we can be holy because He is holy; (2) sacrifice to Him—we are to use our bodies to present personal sacrifices of worship and praise to Him; and (3) service—we are to serve Him and the cause of His kingdom with our bodies.

TEMPLING APPLIED

What is your body? Our world would say it is you. It belongs to you. It should be used to your glory and gratification.

The truth is that when Christ saved us, He purchased us as a dwelling place. "You are not your own, you were bought at a price" (1 Corinthians 6:19-20). As such, our bodies, all that we are, are His. They are where He lives. We really are stewards of God's dwelling place. It is our responsibility and privilege to glorify Him with our bodies.

The principle has profound implication and broad application. Its implication strikes at the very root of our struggle with sin: it is the issue of ownership. Christ has bought us with the price of His own blood. He purchased us from the slave market of sin. Our problem is that we have been unwilling to give up ownership. No longer wanting sin and Satan to own us, we reached out to Christ, and He bought us. We rejoiced. We were thrilled to think He dwelt within us; but we were not so thrilled to realize that His indwelling means ownership, and His presence demands purity, worship, and service. We are housekeepers, care-takers, stewards of His residence. That is not bad. It is a great honor to care for the dwelling place of God. The psalmist had the right perspective when he exclaimed, "I would rather be a doorkeeper in the house of my God than dwell in the tents of the wicked" (Psalm 84:10).

The principle of templing not only carries the profound implication of ownership; it also has a multiplicity of applications. It will affect things like what I eat and drink, how I dress, exercise, sleep, and generally care for myself. It applies to using my body as a means of service by presenting my hands, eyes, feet, lips, mind, and other portions of my being as instruments for His use and for the blessing of others.

Quite simply, the fact that He temples in me demands that I see to it that His residence is clean and pure, that I actively sacrifice in praise and worship to Him, and that I seek ways to use His temple to serve others. As I seek to live out my priority love for Him, I surrender ownership of my body to Christ. It is His. I then become the priest to Guard and serve in His presence. As I seek to discern righteousness, I add to the grid the probing question, What will best serve the reality that God dwells in me?

Two specific applications of the templing principle are highly relevant. One deals with moral purity and the other with the glory of God.

PRIESTS AT THE THRESHOLD

First Corinthians 6:19-20 tackles the problem of sexual immorality. Beginning in verse 13 Paul writes, "The body is not meant for sexual immorality, but for the Lord, and the Lord for the body." He continues in verses 18-19, "Flee from sexual immorality. All other sins a man commits are outside his body, but he who sins sexually sins against his own body. Do you not know that your body is a temple of the Holy Spirit, who is in you, whom you received from God?"

We live in a day of great sexual license. As believers we are bombarded regularly with sensual input. You do not have to go to a sleazy show; advertising on even the most innocent television programs often uses sensual appeal to catch our interest. The other night I found myself wondering if an ad was selling soap or the girl in the tub. I saw more of her than the soap. The music, the mood, the voice on the ad were all produced in sensual tones. A funny atmosphere for a product like soap.

Fashions are often geared to sensual appeal. What our sisters in Christ think looks cute or stylish can create problems for their brothers in Christ. Shorts are shorter, and blouses that used to be opened to the second button are now opened to the third and fourth. Beachwear is tailored to be tantalizing.

Television programming and movie production often include illicit and explicit sexual matter. Soap operas now include more explicit sexual material than prime-time television. The impact is phenomenal. Christians get hooked and end up rooting for someone to have an affair or waiting anxiously for the next sensual sequence. X-rated video cassettes are now easily available. Pornographic magazines are sold in stores in the "nicest" parts of town. Television cable networks offer to bring illicit sexual material into our living rooms.

Our society is strongly geared toward seducing us away from a biblical sense of sexuality and arousing the destructive aspects of our sensual appetites.

It is relevant to note that the templing principle was written to believers in Corinth. Corinth was a key trade town. It was the hub of trade both from east to west and from north to south. Rising from the city was the hill Acropolis, on top of which stood the temple to the goddess Aphrodite. By law, that temple housed no less than one thousand prostitutes who would sell their trade in the city. The temple to Apollo most likely was the center of homosexual activity. The sexual atmosphere was bolstered by the law, the religion, and the populace. Paul wrote this letter to the "church of God in Corinth" (1 Corinthians 1:2) because there was too much Corinth in the church of God.

There may very well be too much of our sexually sinful culture in the church of God today. I fear we have grown numb to the impact. If we have lost our sense of godliness and right-eousness, we are ourselves vulnerable. It is hard to get into a bathtub if the water is too hot. But once you get in, you soon adjust to it—in fact, it feels quite comfortable. Many of God's people bathe in the sexual swamp of our day. It is too hot to handle. We should never become comfortable in it.

God does not want us to deny our sexuality and sensual desires. He created them. Neither, however, does He want us to let them be formed by the input of our culture; He desires that they be exercised within the bounds of what is right. If we do not, the text says we will defile the temple. That is a heavy charge. When the money changers defiled the Temple in Christ's day with their greed, they were not chased out be-cause they sold in the Temple. They were chased out because they were charging exorbitant prices for sacrificial animals and for the exchange of foreign currency. They were taking financial advantage of pilgrims who came to worship God. Christ dramatically turned their tables and dispelled them from the Temple with their greed. God does not take lightly the defilement of His temple.

What then shall we do? We must stand as priests at the thresholds of our temples to guard against the intrusion of moral defilement. It is our responsibility as royal priests to guard the thresholds of our eyes, our ears, our minds, our hands, our total bodies. We who have become one in the spirit with the indwelling Christ must not become one with another in sexual sin (1 Corinthians 6:15-17).

We should not refuse the defiling sexual input of our world simply because someone told us it was bad. We should remain pure because we love God and seek to guard against anything that would defile and desecrate His temple. That principle will apply itself in a multitude of ways and provide strength to be a free-standing wall of moral purity for the sake of His temple and the honor of His name.

GOD LIVES HERE

The second application of the templing principle relates to the honor and glory of God. The conclusion of Paul's discussion of the templing principle is, "therefore, honor God with your body" (1 Corinthians 6:20).

People in our neighborhood know that I am a minister. As such I represent Christianity to them. Periodically I note a car slowing down as it passes my house. I recognize the occupants as some of the flock. I can almost hear them telling their friends in the back seat, "Our pastor lives here."

All of that encourages me to keep my house and yard in good shape. It is a reflection on my Lord and my position as a pastor. No one in our neighborhood has dandelions. So each spring I make an annual trip the hardware store for "weed and feed." Then early one morning I put it the into my spreader and walk back and forth, carefully watching my tracks in the dew so my lawn does not end up looking like the flag. We rake our leaves and pull our weeds, not just because we like to have a well-kept place but, more important, because it is a reflection on our relationship to Christ.

Paul says it is like that with the temple principle. God lives here! My body is His home, and He seeks to use it to bring glory to His reputation in this world. God created us as image-bearers (Genesis 1:26-27) so that we might have the capacity to be reflections of His character. We are to be moving reflections of His love, mercy, righteousness, justice, patience, holiness, and grace. Glorifying God simply means to be a reflector so that the world may see the reality of the invisible God who is really there. God dwells in us and we are to show that with our bodies. If it is the place where God lives, then it should look like God lives there.

This principle will apply in what we wear, what we eat, in the words that come out of our mouths, in fitness, where we go, and a host of other situations.

There is a great cartoon that shows a rather chubby, forlorn figure in a bathrobe and shower cap, standing on the scale. Dejectedly he says, "My body is not my temple; it's my garage." I immediately thought about my garage. It is the place where we put everything for which we have no place. Before long the clutter is unbelievable. Frankly, there have been times when I have been ashamed to open my garage. My neighbor keeps his fastidiously in order, and our garages face each other. I soon get so sick of the clutter that I dedicate a Saturday to cleaning it up. By the end of the day the clutter is gone. I feel so good that I would like to leave the garage door open for a week to let everyone see how the Stowells keep their garage!

I wonder if God feels as though our bodies, His residences, are more like garages than temples. We accumulate a lot of clutter from the world. We often think we can hide it by covering up on the outside. But eventually it shows. It is impossible to have bad input without eventually having bad output. Knowing that our bodies are where God lives should motivate us to clean out the clutter. Take a spiritual workday and discard thoughts of bitterness. Bag and throw away the old patterns of sexual fantasy. Put memories in their proper place. Organize attitudes. Leave it clean to the core. We should live so that we could leave the door open for all to see.

In fact, it might be a good discipline to envision a sign around our necks that says in big letters, "God Lives Here." I think we would think, act and react in a new light if that sign were visible for all to see. Can you imagine purchasing a pornographic magazine while wearing a sign like that? How about attacking someone verbally? It might even alter the way we act in heavy traffic.

Standing as priests at the threshold, guarding the purity of God's place, and reflecting on the fact that God lives in us provide strong influences for true righteousness from within. What better way could we say to God that we love Him than to keep His temple clean and consistent with His glory? What better way could we surrender to Him than to surrender our bodies, our entire beings, to His ownership? A commitment to the templing principle will provide a standard for discernment in the midst of great unrighteousness.

> What agreement is there between the temple of God and idols? For we are the temple of the living God. As God has said, "I will live with them and walk among them, and I will be their God, and they will be my people." "Therefore come out from among them and be ye separate," says the Lord. "Touch no unclean thing and I will receive you. I will be a Father to you, and you will be my sons and my daughters," Says the Lord Almighty. (2 Corinthians 6:16-18)

7

Loving Our Neighbor:
The Principle of True Love

People are both a delight and a distraction. They light up our lives and leave us lonely. They both complement and complicate. People are precious; people are problems. People provide places of refuge and points of conflict. They encourage and exasperate us. They misunderstand us, make us feel responsible, judge us, and use us. They demand that we be flexible, tolerant, and adjusting.

Christ says that the second great command is to *"love your neighbor as yourself"* (Matthew 22:39, italics added). If we are truly interested in expressing our love to God by surrendering to Him then our first point of surrender is to the people God has allowed in our lives. I want to say, "Lord, let's start my love for You someplace else. I'll tithe. I'll witness. I'll even teach a Sunday school class. I'd be willing to *think about* the mission field. But love my neighbor? That's a bad place to start. You see, Lord, I don't think you know my neighbor real well. How about suggesting something else?" And He would say, "No. The place to start loving Me is by loving your neighbor."

WHAT IT MEANS

Two basic questions must be answered if we are to actualize this command into genuine righteousness: What does it mean to love in the context of my relationship to others? and Who is my neighbor?

First, what is the essence of loving others? The Greek word for "love" in this passage is the same word used in the first command, to love God. It carries the same essential meaning of yielding, surrendering, or giving. But because it is to be exercised toward other people, it carries a different kind of application. Whereas loving God means surrendering to His will, loving others is more aptly applied to yielding to their needs. That is graphically seen in verses like John 3:16 and Romans 5:8. In those texts, God's love actualizes itself in two dimensions. There is first a *sensitivity* to our need. The world has a need (John 3:16). It is hopelessly lost in the problem of sin, unable to help itself. The "us" in Romans 5:8 is defined as we who are sinners. Being first sensitive to the need, Christ then *sacrificed* from His resources to meet the need. Christ died for us. That sacrifice was the necessary outgrowth of God's choice to express love toward us. Love cannot be complete if both components, sensitivity and sacrifice, are not in place.

Understanding love in that way demands that we reverse the tendency of the flesh and begin to live with an "others orientation." As Paul writes to the Philippians,

> Make my joy complete by being like-minded, having the same love, being one in spirit and purpose. Do nothing out of selfish ambition or vain conceit, but in humility consider others better than yourselves. Each of you should look not only to your own interests, but also to the interests of others. Your attitude should be the same as that of Christ Jesus: who, being in very nature God, did not consider equality with God something to be grasped, but made himself nothing, taking the very nature of a servant, being made in human likeness. And being found in appearance as a man, he

humbled himself and became obedient to death, even death on a cross. (Philippians 2:2-8)

Knowing the meaning of the command moves us to the second key question, Who is my neighbor? Because the command is rooted in the Old Testament (Leviticus 19:18), it would be well to understand what the Old Testament meant by "neighbor." In essence it meant *anyone who enters the arena of my existence.* It meant strangers, the Gentiles who had converted to Judaism, friends, family, and those who lived nearby. The Pharisees sought to get Christ's opinion as to who their neighbor was, and He included even enemies as He told the story of the Good Samaritan. In fact, in that parable Christ illustrates that anyone in need, friend or foe, is a neighbor. And He concludes that neighborly love is showing sacrificial mercy on those whom we can help.

Why It Is Tough

Integrating the mind of Christ into our existence, the attitude that is both sensitive and sacrificial to the needs of others, is a challenge that must be faced on three fronts: the challenge from within, the challenge from our culture, and the challenge of our neighbor.

Initially it will be difficult to love others because of our *sinful bent to self.* Let me hasten to note that self is not bad. In fact, in these foundational commands self is couched in terms of high esteem. Self is the treasure that I give to God as I love Him with sweet surrender. Self is the gift I give to others as I sensitively sacrifice to meet their need. Self only becomes sinful when it is spent on self. In fact, all sin begins with doing what self wants to do for self. The flesh always bends the arrows of my energies back toward me so that I seek to serve the big "I." Christ's way is exactly the opposite. It means taking the arrows of my resources, energies, and possessions and by the Spirit's power directing them toward those around my life.

The challenge from within must be continually checked until we are at last skilled in the art and joy of being a blessing to others.

The challenge from within gains ammunition from *the world without*. Our cultural ethic contradicts the kingdom understanding of both ourselves and others. The prevailing ethic of our day begins with "Me." Self-fulfillment is the pivotal motivation for many. Tragically, many of us bring that deadly baggage on board our pilgrimage for Christ. And although we claim to be reflections of His love, we remain essentially committed to "Me." The cultural doctrine then produces, as a natural by-product, a new definition of others. If "I" am all-important, then others are not as important as I. Others become pawns on the chessboard of my life. They exist to bring joy and fulfillment to me, to help make me successful, to provide for my social acceptance and peer encouragement. Others are the means by which I get rid of loneliness. They are the people I am seen with. They become that which I climb on, play with, and push out of the way.

Not only are people redefined in a me-first world, but things become elevated to a position of exaggerated worth. Material objects easily seduce us in our inebriation with self. They offer, though it is sheer deceit, happiness, prestige, joy, and fulfillment. The end result of it all is that things become more significant to us than people. Opportunities to gain things drive us to work longer, which then takes us away from our families, churches, and meaningful time with others. If we see people as a means to the end of gaining more things, we will use them, deceive them, and misrepresent them—all to get and gain in the temple of materialism.

In a "me first, things second, people third" world, others are not a priority. Our neighbor becomes neglected, used, and abused.

The remaining challenge to our love for others is the *nature of people themselves*. There are those who may not deserve our sensitivity, much less our sacrifice. Some are caught up in playing games. There are the manipulators, the intimidators, the guilt-inducers. We hesitate to get too close lest we are caught in their web. There are always some who seek to take advantage, some who seek to possess, and others who will love us and leave us. Some of us have been scarred by past relationships and fear running the risk again.

In the face of all of this Christ asks us to reach out to others. It is not that He is unaware of the difficulty of the task. He came and loved when it meant great sacrifice to self, when it required that He would minister to a world that rarely would reach back and minister to Him—a world that would use Him, misunderstand Him, malign, and crucify Him; a fickle world that loved Him and left Him. His example helps us cut through the challenges of our own self-centeredness, the world without, and the way others behave.

Making It Work

Consistency in our love toward others demands special strength. We need a unique motivation. The strength to love our neighbor comes from the fact that this command is the corollary to the first great command. I love others because I love God. He is the ultimate priority in my life and as such sends me on a mission of love. The power of my alignment to Him crumbles the barriers and deflates every challenge.

If we are motivated to meet others' needs for reasons less than our love for God, then our love will vacillate and depend on external situations and pressures. If a wife waits until her husband deserves her love, she may wait a long time. If, however, she is personally committed to an internal love for God, then she will love her husband regardless. Husbands, if committed to loving God, will sensitively meet the needs of their wives even on those days of nagging and unreasonableness. In fact, our love for the Father provides enough motivation to go so far as to "Love your enemies and pray for those who persecute you, that you may be the sons of your Father in heaven" (Matthew 5:44-45).

Christ's love for us was motivated by His commitment to the Father. He certainly did not love us because we deserved it or because He felt like loving us. He came to do His Father's will, and that meant that He would love us with His life.

How Does It Happen?

The text illustrates the way in which this love is to happen. We have already discovered the key motivation in neighborly love, which is surrender to God. Therefore, we love for His sake whether people deserve it or not. Having discovered that agapē love is a choice and not a feeling, we give our love to others as an act of our will. We decide to love whether we feel like it or not.

Christ explicitly describes the pattern of this love by adding that we are to love others *as we love ourselves* (Matthew 22:39).

How do we love ourselves? *Tenderly* and *eagerly.* I was once fixing an appliance for my family and feeling quite frustrated about the experience. The hair dryer must have been built so that normal people could not repair it. The first step was to unscrew the screws that held it together. They were set down tiny shafts about one-half inch deep into the appliance. My Phillips screwdriver proved inadequate for the task, so I got out my pocket knife with the tiny blade. It fit nicely down the shaft, but as it bit into the slots on the screw I began to turn the knife. The screw wouldn't budge. I pressed harder and turned with more force. As I did the knife folded and my finger, caught between the handle and the blade, was sliced with a neat gash almost to the bone.

Did I look at my finger and think, *You're too much trouble. I have work to do. You'll have to wait?*

Not on your life.

I dropped what I was doing, grabbed my finger, and ran into the kitchen. My family, witnessing the crisis, followed me like ducklings behind a mother duck. My wife turned on the water to rinse out the wound. Taking good care of myself, I said, "Not too hot, not too cold." Then they went to dress it and put a bandage on it. I reminded them not to put the bandage over any hairs on my finger because I didn't want to have to rip it off, causing additional pain.

I cared for myself with tender insight, sensitivity, and eagerness. That is how we are to love others.

The Righteous Result

As I internalize the commitment to love my neighbor as an expression of my love for God, I actualize it by becoming sensitive to others' needs and then sharing my resources to meet their needs. In what ways do the the following two commands produce righteousness?

The answer is simple, clear, and powerful.

If I love you I will not lie to you. Lying is most often a tactic used to gain advantage over another, to deceive, manipulate or hurt another. It leaves my neighbor with weakened resources.

In dating, being sensitive to the needs of the other means sacrificing sensual desires to meet his or her needs. Our dates need to have hearts that are free of guilt, worry, and fear. They need a strong sense of self-worth and a clear conscience to experience God's best. Disciplining ourselves morally for their benefit will accomplish what is best and righteousness will prevail.

If I love you I will not covet your wife, your goods, or your gain. I will rejoice when you rejoice instead of coveting when you prosper.

Loving others will keep us from adultery, stealing, manipulation, and a host of other social sins.

Loving my neighbor will require forgiving my neighbor. It only serves self to be bitter and seek revenge.

Loving others will encourage modest dress and modest actions. It will refuse to tease and incite immoral thoughts in another's heart. It will keep us from pornography, which alters our view of people and ultimately affects our relationships with them. Instead of viewing others as precious individuals, pornography presents women as sex objects to be used by men and gives the viewer a warped perspective that leads to damaging and sinful attitudes.

Most powerfully, our love for others will not only produce righteousness by keeping us from sin, but it will produce a positive surge of righteousness in our lives as well. A commitment to loving my wife will lead me to become sensitive to her needs, to spend time with her, to listen to her attentively, to share in the responsibilities at home, and to fill her life with those special surprises that bring her joy. It will drive me to be a caring and compassionate father. It will totally alter my friendships. Instead of wondering what my friends can do for me, I will ask what I can do for them. It will drive me to an active concern for widows, the helpless, the fatherless. It will, perhaps most significantly, catapult me into evangelism as I sense the eternal needs of my neighbors and reach out to them with the truth.

This command is used throughout the New Testament as the key to genuine righteousness. Paul writes in Romans 13:8-10,

> Let no debt remain outstanding, except the continuing debt to love one another, for he who loves his fellow-man has fulfilled the law. The commandments, "Do not commit adultery," "Do not murder," "Do not steal," "Do not covet," *and whatever other commandments there may be,* are summed up in this one rule: "Love your neighbor as yourself." Love does no harm to its neighbor. Therefore love is the fulfillment of the law. (Italics added)

To the Galatians he wrote,

> You, my brothers, were called to be free. But do not use your freedom to indulge the sinful nature; rather, serve one

another in love. The entire law is summed up in a single command: "Love your neighbor as yourself." If you keep on biting and devouring each other, watch out or you will be destroyed by each other. (Galatians 5:13-15)

And James, in reproving those who showed preference to the rich stated, "If you really keep the royal law found in Scripture, 'Love your neighbor as yourself,' you are doing right. But if you show favoritism, you sin and are convicted by the law as lawbreakers'" (James 2:8-9).

8

Loving Our Neighbor: The Principle of Otherness

A young boy's sister was in desperate need of a blood transfusion. Because of her rare blood type, he was one of the few potential donors. He consented. As he lay on the table giving blood for the first time in his little life he said to the nurse, "How long will it be before I die?" She quickly explained that giving blood would not kill him. Nevertheless, he had been willing to love his sister even with his life.

Within the family of God our love has a special and significant application. It is in fact God's specially designed principle to not only produce righteousness but to unite and solidify His Body in the midst of a hostile world.

At the close of His ministry, Christ made a special application of the "love your neighbor" principle of Matthew 22:39. He spoke of it as an activity that was to be practiced *first* among those who are a part of God's family. He then gave a clear example of how that love is to be exercised by encouraging His disciples to love one another in the same way that He loved them. That intensification of the love principle is found in John 13:34-35, where Christ says, "A new commandment I give you: Love one another. As I have loved you, so you must love one another. By this all men will know that you are my disciples, if you love one another." The newness of this command lies in two realities that are different from the old command.

First, we are to exercise the principle of love within the Body of Christ. That does not cancel the old responsibility to our neighbor, but it does prioritize the command to those in the family of God. It may be what Paul had in mind when he wrote to the Galatians, "Therefore, as we have opportunity, let us do good to all people, especially to those who belong to the family of believers" (Galatians 6:10).

Given the hostile environment that the disciples were soon to face, mutual caring would become of utmost importance.

Second, we have not only the model of our love for ourselves, but we now have a better model; we are to love in the way that Christ demonstrated love to His disciples. He is the ultimate model. We learn several key aspects of mutual love from Christ's example.

Christ loved *intrinsically*. He is love; therefore, He does love. His love for His disciples was not a response to them. It was prompted internally, out of His heart of love. We usually love for something, because of something, or to gain something. Our love for each other must not be a response, but a gift based on the fact that "God has poured out his love into our hearts by the Holy Spirit, whom he has given us" (Romans 5:5). Our call is not to be responders but initiators when it comes to love.

Christ also loved with a *servant's heart*. Just before He shared this "new command," the Lord had captured the disciples' attention by doing something unique in the upper room where they were arguing among themselves about who would be the greatest in the kingdom (Luke 22:24). Because it was a borrowed room, no servant had met them at the door to wash their feet, which was a common act of hospitality. While they were discussing position and power, who would ever be willing to do such a menial task for his fellow disciples? If John had asked Peter to get some water and a towel and wash their feet, Peter might have said, "Do I look like a servant to you?"

In the midst of all of that the Lord of Lords and King of Kings, the Creator of the universe, rises, drops His robe, puts a towel around His waist as a servant would, and washes their feet. He then calls them to the same attitude.

In our world of status and prestige, of Gucci bags, designer jeans, and polo players embroidered on shirts, God looks for the heart of a servant who is not seeking power and prestige but opportunities to help and empower others. Christ called us to a servant's identity when He taught his disciples,

> The rulers of the Gentiles lord it over them, and their high officials exercise authority over them. Not so with you. Instead, whoever wants to become great among you must be your servant, and whoever wants to be first must be your slave—just as the Son of Man did not come to be served, but to serve, and to give his life as a ransom for many. (Matthew 20:25-28)

Christ also loved *regardless of socio-economic background.* The disciples were an interesting mix of people. Matthew was a tax collector; three were fishermen. There were rich and poor in their midst. Christ cared for them equally. Some are prone to care for the rich out of sheer self-interest: "Perhaps if we love them, they will like us; to be seen with them would be a real plus!" Or we may scorn the rich: "Who do they think they are, driving a car like that to church?"

Before God all are of equal value, and all have needs that deserve our love and concern. Christ always saw beyond the surface to the real issues of life, and He loved regardless.

Christ loved *regardless of temperament problems.* Peter was impetuous, always ready for verbal commitment but rarely ready to follow through. Thomas was a doubter, a skeptic. People's personalities can be an irritation at times. There are always a few people around that are hard to like. I don't think Christ liked Peter's lack of commitment. He certainly did not like Thomas's doubting spirit. The Bible says that without faith it is impossible to please God (Hebrews 11:6)!

Do you think Christ *loved* Peter and Thomas? Absolutely. What an important lesson to learn: we do not have to like people to love them. In fact, they may be unlovable because few people have ever cared about them. Perhaps they have known only abuse. Our love may be the beginning of transformation in their lives. It is our privilege to be what Christ would be to them. Although we may not be able to be their best friends, we can be a source of caring and concern.

Christ loved with His *time and talents*. He often took His time with the sick, the children, the disciples, even the Pharisees. He invested His time in teaching them, healing them, encouraging and reproving them. His eternal talents were spent on their behalf. Awakened abruptly in the middle of the night, with the boat on which he was sleeping threatened by a storm, He responded to the anxious pleas of His disciples for help and marshalled His supernatural gifts to meet their needs as He stilled the wind and the waves. We all have an inventory of resources in our lives. We have time to give, talents to share, a listening ear, a comforting smile, a hug, a bag of groceries, a meal, our prayers of intercession, an "I love you." Those are all within easy grasp and are the arsenal of love that we each possess.

Christ also loved us by *giving up some of His privileges* to be able to exercise His love for us. As Paul states, "Who, being in very nature God, did not consider equality with God something to be grasped, but made himself nothing, taking the very nature of a servant, being made in human likeness" (Philippians 2:6-7).

Christ gave up many of His heavenly prerogatives to love us. When love is sacrificial, it demonstrates its true depth. What we are willing to give up for someone reflects the quality of our love for them.

WHEN PUSH COMES TO SHOVE

Love is most difficult to give when it demands that we give up a preference, a liberty, something that is special to us. Yet living together does demand some sacrifice. One of my children mastered the finely-tuned skill of chewing gum and making it pop. I hate to sound intolerant but it drives me bats! Living together in peace demands that someone makes a sacrifice. I, of course, think that the gum-popper should quit; my child thinks I ought to be more tolerant.

It is funny—sad may be a better word—how little things can become divisive. Unfortunately, intolerance and imposing our preferences on others can divide and defeat even the best of Christian groups. God's Word says that our love for each other is the one thing that will lift us above all of that. It is a matter of making love more important than preference, privilege, or liberty.

By the time our third baby came along we were able to afford disposable diapers. What a pleasure to be able to simply throw the old diaper away and put on a clean one. When it came to changing the baby it was important to know exactly what was disposable. How ridiculous it would have been to dispose of the baby along with the diaper. Naturally, I never did that. That would have been unthinkable. The baby had value; the diaper did not.

I wish that we were that clear in our thinking as we relate to our fellow believers. We seem to have a difficult time sorting out what is worth clinging to and what can be disposed. The problem does not involve clearly revealed statements about righteousness, such as "thou shalt not murder," but rather falls into those areas about which well-meaning Christians disagree. We must deal with preferences, issues of what is and what is not allowable before God in the context of our love for one another.

THE POWER OF PREFERENCES

We tend to feel strongly about our preferences. We all have our views of what Christians should and should not do. Those are often grounded in our upbringing, our cultural setting, our personal experiences, and our particular temperaments or spiritual gifts. Therefore our preferences tend to come with strong emotional support, making them even more difficult to deal with. Some preferences are even held as being standards of biblical spirituality. Others are issues of what we feel are our God-given rights in the liberty that He has afforded us. When Christians come together, inevitably preferences clash.

Love is the only solution. It is the glue that keeps us together.

Committing ourselves to that which is most important, knowing what is and what is not disposable, brings us out of the war of preferences to peace and power as we live and work together for Christ.

Both the church at Corinth and the church at Rome reflected this tension. Paul wrote to the Roman believers,

> Accept him whose faith is weak, without passing judgment on disputable matters. One man's faith allows him to eat everything, but another man, whose faith is weak, eats only vegetables. The man who eats everything must not look down on him who does not, and the man who does not eat everything must not condemn the man who does, for God has accepted him. Who are you to judge someone else's servant? To his own master he stands or falls. And he will stand, for the Lord is able to make him stand. One man considers one day more sacred than another; another man considers every day alike. Each one should be fully convinced in his own mind. He who regards one day as special, does so to the Lord. He who eats meat, eats to the Lord, for he gives thanks to God; and he who abstains, does so to the Lord and gives thanks to God. For none of us lives to himself alone and none of us dies to himself alone. If we live, we live to the Lord; and if we die, we die to the Lord. So, whether we live or die, we belong to the Lord. (Romans 14:1-8)

Three issues of preference were troubling the church at Rome: sacred days, which probably refers to Jewish Holy Days or to the keeping of certain strict sabbath rules (v. 5); eating meat, which refers to both the Old Testament ceremonial laws on unclean meat and meat offered to idols in the pagan temples (vv. 2, 6); and drinking of wine (vv. 17, 21).

JUDGE NOT

In the face of conflicting preferences Paul initially instructs the Romans to refuse to judge one another because each must give a personal account to God. He writes,

> For this reason, Christ died and returned to life so that he might be the Lord of both the dead and the living. You, then, why do you judge your brother? Or why do you look down on your brother? For we will all stand before God's judgment seat. It is written: "'As surely as I live,' says the Lord, 'every knee will bow before me; every tongue will confess to God.'" So then, each of us will give an account of himself to God. (Romans 14:9-12)

The application of the principle is not that we give up our preferences because of people who judge our behavior. People bound by code systems are prone to criticize and spiritually devalue those who do not fit their code. The text does not ask anyone to give up his liberty for the sake of a judgmental brother. Actually it demands that one give up his judgmental ways and stop using his preferences as a spiritual whipping post for others. If one brother holds one set of applications, he must give room for others to hold their set of applications. They are not ultimately accountable for each other but are individually accountable to God. Love in action makes us mature enough to work together in spite of differing preferences.

The injunction against being judgmental works both ways. Those who lean toward a more liberated life-style tend to judge some as being narrow legalists or old-fashioned. That is just as wrong as when those holding a more restricted view of behavior call those who are more open fleshly and carnal.

What the text does demand is that I yield my preferences when the exercise of those preferences causes a brother or sister to fall or to have their spiritual progress impeded (Romans 14:13).

There are two issues that determine whether or not I should give up my liberty for the greater cause of love for my brother. The first issue is my impact on what the text calls our "weaker" brother. We tend to think of someone who is "weak" as being of less worth than others. We must first discover that the weaker Christian is not of less value. Our weaker brother is not a second-class citizen any more than the "weaker" partner in 1 Peter 3:7 is of less value. The weaker brother is not someone who holds a more restrictive set of personal preferences. The presence of a weaker brother should not be an occasion for us to cater to the flesh, either from arrogance or from the assumption that stronger is better. The weaker one, the one we defer to, is one who is unable to do what we do with a clear conscience and who would be tempted to violate his conscience under the influence of our participation in a particular activity (Romans 14:13, 22-23). When a man violates his conscience to do something, he falls spiritually and sins, because he does not do it in faith toward God (14:23). The text demands that I not encourage his sin by my behavior.

We each have a fence around our lives designed to keep us from falling into sin. It is what the text calls our faith. It forms our conscience. It has certain preferences woven into it, and it keeps us living at peace with ourselves and with our God. Climbing over it establishes a bad precedent. If we break through once for a particular activity, it will become increasingly easy to break through for other, perhaps more dangerous things. The text says if our conscience is not clear, if we cannot do something in faith, it is sin, and we should not do it.

Therefore Paul says that if you believe it is right to do something that a brother cannot do, "whatever you believe about these things keep between yourself and God" (Romans 14:22). It is your secret. Do not flaunt it. If you exercise your liberty as you fellowship with him, it may intimidate the brother who cannot do it. He may yield just to appear "in" or "broad" or to avoid personal rejection.

Practically speaking, we exercise love toward our brother when, while fellowshiping with him, we restrict any of our own liberties that might encourage him to break his faith toward God. As Paul wrote, we must not do anything that will cause our brother to fall (Romans 14:21). Paul concluded, "We who are strong ought to bear with the failings of the weak and not to please ourselves. Each of us should please his neighbor for his good, to build him up" (Romans 15:1-2). That is exactly what love would demand.

I have often wished I had the day back that I encouraged a friend to do something with me that I felt free to do in Christ. He did not sense that freedom. He did it anyway and was unhappy the whole time. In fact, because he could not do it in faith toward God I actually led him to sin. I loved myself and spiritually harmed him. I learned then that my love for him should have outweighed my personal preferences.

The second issue addressed by the text is that of eliminating anything that is going to cause some measure of harm to my fellow believer. Paul wrote, "If your brother is distressed because of what you eat, you are no longer acting in love. Do not by your eating destroy your brother for whom Christ died" (Romans 14:15).

Interestingly, the text applies this principle to the use of alcohol as a beverage (14:21). Granted, upon study of the Scriptures, many find solid biblical grounds for total abstinence. Yet there are growing numbers of believers who have placed drinking in the liberty category of their walk with Christ. Unfortunately, sectors of the Body of Christ have become polarized and divided over preferences to drink or not to drink. It is appropriate to ask ourselves how a commitment to the priority of love shapes a biblical response. Several questions are appropriate.

Does the use of alcohol violate a commitment of *love toward my children?* Could alcohol be a destructive force in their lives? Studies demonstrate that some people have a greater propensity toward alcohol abuse than others. It is possible that a child in my home may have that tendency. With all the potential destruction that alcohol can produce in a life, it is imperative that, as a parent, I measure my example and its impact on the future well-being of my children. It is often true that "What one generation allows in moderation the next will allow in excess." As parents we will function as an example or an excuse.

Does the use of alcohol violate my commitment of *love toward my fellow believers?* There are Christians in nearly every fellowship who are struggling to get rid of the bondage of alcohol. Would my abstinence be an encouragement to them? Would my use of alcohol be an excuse for them and lend support to their bondage? Does my use of alcoholic beverages limit personal fellowship? Some time ago a group of Christians were having a dinner party and structured the guest list to include only those who drank wine. That is a sad standard for fellowship; some who needed fellowship and love were excluded simply because they did not drink.

As a pastor, Sunday school teacher, or other spiritual leader, *will my use of alcohol hinder my ability to edify those who are under my ministry?* Would some be closed to my teaching if they knew that I drank? Will my use of alcohol encourage those who do not drink because of conscience toward God to break their "faith" toward Him? Do we want the teens of our church to assume that they can drink because of our example?

A man sat in my office recently and told me how he had become spiritually defeated because of drinking. He recalled that it had begun when his Christian friend encouraged him to drink with him while on an outing. Another said that he drank with friends who were fellow Christians and all the time felt wrong on the inside. He was violating his faith and breaking down his conscience.

Those kinds of real life situations should give rise to serious evaluation of the use of alcohol in the context of our Christian love for one another.

THINGS MORE IMPORTANT

The reason for sacrificing my liberty is that there are spiritual commodities that are more important than any preferred activities. In the passage Paul mentions five non-disposable realities that outweigh our preferences. As we have learned, the first is our *commitment to love*. Paul teaches us that if what we are doing harms our brother then we are no longer acting in love toward him (Romans 14:15). Love always protects (1 Corinthians 13:7). Love is willing to sacrifice personal privilege for another's safety and benefit (John 3:16; Ephesians 5:25).

He adds to the list of more important things *righteousness, peace,* and *joy* (Romans 14:17). The text indicates that those are non-negotiable essentials of the kingdom of God. They are of far superior worth than personal preferences or, as the text says, "eating and drinking." When my influence on another destroys his sense of personal righteousness, peace with both God and himself; when my activities rob the fellowship of their sense of joy, then I have devalued the currency of the kingdom and have inflated the lower values of my personal preferences.

"Mutual edification" is also mentioned as something of greater worth than my preferences (Romans 14:19). When I was invited to speak at a conference of missionaries in Puerto Rico, my host asked if my wife would refrain from wearing slacks because the culture there identified women in slacks with immorality. He said it would be offensive to our sisters in Christ. We gladly changed our wardrobe plans. The effectiveness of our opportunity to strengthen and edify fellow Christians was of far greater weight than my wife's privilege to wear slacks.

Disarming conflict in the body when it comes to differences in our preferences means weighing certain considerations carefully.

1. Do I have a judgmental spirit toward those who differ?
2. Can I do this and still live in love toward those who differ?
3. Will this activity encourage some to break their conscience toward God and do something that they cannot do in good faith?
4. Will it cause others some measure of harm or defeat in their pilgrimage?
5. Will it promote or hinder righteousness, peace, and joy in the assembly?
6. Will it inhibit or preclude my ability to edify another believer?

Free to Love

In essence, the application of the principle means that love is of higher priority than my assumed freedoms in Christ. As Paul told the Galatians,

> You, my brothers, were called to be free. But do not use your freedom to indulge the sinful nature; rather, serve one another in love." The entire law is summed up in a single command. "Love your neighbor as yourself." If you keep on biting and devouring each other watch out or you will be destroyed by each other. (Galatians 6:13-15)

It Makes a Difference

Loving our brothers and sisters in Christ will produce not only continuing unity but an intense righteousness as well. If every thought, act, and attitude were weighed in the light of our brother's well-being, our churches and relationships would be transformed. Critical, destructive talk would be eliminated. Judgmental spirits would melt. We would seek to understand and help each other instead of destroying each other. We would give more freely, serve more readily, reach out more tenderly. Friendships and fellowship would be deepened. Preferences would cease to be destructive. We would become wonderfully bonded together to face a hostile alien world with the power of Christ.

Not only does loving one another produce a bond of righteousness, it also demonstrates that we belong to God. Christ said, "By this all men will know that you are my disciples, *if you love one another*" (John 13:35). He does not say they will know because we "don't drink, dance, smoke, chew, or go with girls that do." As important as genuine biblical convictions may be, they do not necessarily make us distinct. It would be foolish to get on an airplane, sit in the non-smoking section, and assume that everyone else there belonged to Christ. A friend of mine who was saved in his thirties had never touched liquor. He had seen it devastate his father. His abstinence had nothing to do with his relationship to Christ.

There is only one thing that makes us *truly* distinct in this self-serving, self-gratifying world, and that is a Christ-like sense of concern that is willing to sacrifice for another's benefit. Only those who have been to the foot of the cross, who have been loved with that unconditional love from God shed abroad in our hearts, have the capacity to consistently reach out. It is the way we are known to be His.

In fact, not only will we be known as Christians by our love, but as God's people become a caring community with an intense sense of interest in each other's needs, it will generate a powerful attraction to Christ. In all of the world's self-centeredness, many are becoming more and more isolated, more lonely, looking for someone to care for them. Locked into a ghetto of one, they begin to search for someone who will reach out to rescue them. A church that really cares will draw the lost who are longing for love. It was often said of the first-century church by those who saw them live, "How they love one another." Community love among God's people cuts an important path of pre-evangelism.

A true commitment to the importance of love will drive us to excellent choices, choices that will benefit others and glorify God.

9

Excellence:
The Principle of Choices

His name was Tom Wilson. A newspaper clipping about him was sitting on my desk. It was a sad, tragic story. Tom was a member of "The Third Reich," a neo-Nazi motorcycle gang in Detroit. He and his girl friend had just parked their cycle in front of a drug store. A van drove by, slowed down, the window lowered, and a machine gun pulverized Tom's body with eight bullets. Tom fell to the sidewalk, a victim of gang warfare.

I set down the clipping, wondering why it had been put on my desk, as the name was unfamiliar to me. It was not until the church business manager walked into the office that I learned the connection.

He unfolded an amazing scenario. Tom Wilson's parents had been pillars in our church. Tom had grown up attending with them and had been baptized in our church. He had been faithful in Sunday school and active in the high school youth group.

I leaned back in my chair and thought, *How can it be? How do you get from here to a bloodied sidewalk?* I knew the answer to my questions.

Choices.

They are serious business.

Choices determine direction. My train set was my boyhood delight. Along the track I had several switch tracks. Those tracks would set the direction for the oncoming train. If you set them in proper sequence you could totally change the direction of the train.

Choices are the switches of our lives. A friend once told me that our lives are not made by the dreams we dream but by the choices we make. How very true. Who we are, where we are, and what we are is a composite of a hundred dozen choices we have made. For Tom, it was probably not a choice to walk out of his youth group and join a hostile motorcycle gang. More likely it was many small choices. A choice to do what he wanted to do. A choice to rebel in a small, insignificant way. A choice of a friend. In time his life was re-routed and finally derailed.

Choices reveal where we really are on the inside. When we are locked into closed systems of behavior where all the choices are made for us and sufficient pressure is placed on us to conform, we rarely have the opportunity to even know for ourselves where we are spiritually. When given the liberty to make personal choices, they reveal who we really are and where we are in the maturity process. The true level of our righteousness is best revealed in the choices made that no one will know about.

Choices are controllable. Each of us is in clear control of our choices. Even when we are placed in situations where we are in some sense victimized by others' choices, we still are in control of how we respond. Because choices are determinative in our lives it is significant that we control them properly. In one sense we really do master our own destiny. Those who hide behind "I can't help myself," "My parents are at fault," "I've always been this way," "If you only knew my husband,"

and comments of that ilk are only deceiving themselves. In reality they have chosen to respond in an irresponsible way. We control our choices and therefore are responsible for the choices we make.

Choices cause ripples. Most of us have at one time or another tried to skip stones across the placid surface of a lake or pond. I used to like to count the skips. One . . . two . . . five . . . ten! Each time the stones hit the water tiny waves would impact the tranquillity of the lake around it. It is like that with choices. Each choice we make either blesses those around us or creates grief and trouble. Even choices made in secret, choices within the walls of our mind, choices when we are all alone, determine what we are becoming, and that in turn will alter how we treat and react to others.

EXCELLENT CHOICES

Actually this book is about choices, heart choices that emanate from Christ at the core of our being; choices not externally imposed but internally generated from the personal ownership of basic principles that God has established for our lives; choices that are a result of running life decisions through the grid of biblical principles; choices that produce righteousness through an actualized love for God and a love for others.

Paul calls these kinds of choices "excellent." He states that when our love abounds in knowledge and discernment we are able to *discern what is best.* The King James version translates, "that ye may approve things that are excellent" (Philippians 1:10).

It would be great if life were simple enough to be divided between that which is good and bad. Unfortunately life is somewhat more complicated than that. There actually is a whole continuum of choices. Some choices are rotten; others are bad. Choices can be average or even good. Rotten choices are those made with total disregard for their possible devastation to ourselves or others. Bad choices, like rotten choices, are those that clearly violate biblical principles. Average choices paint our lives in the drab colors of mediocrity. They are the "Well, a lot of people I know do it!" choices. Good choices are choices that basically have the support of community and biblical values.

But God's Word adds one more category to the spectrum of our choices. It is the *best* or *excellent* choice. Paul recommends that we put the "excellent" to the test (Philippians 1:10). The word translated to "discern" is a word that was used by the Greeks when they spoke of testing coins to discern if they were genuine or not. Paul says, in essence, that we should put excellence to the test. It is a call to prove the value of the things that are truly best.

As Christians we are prone to experiment with things that are marginal. We like to play at the fences, to peek through and then climb over them. A life committed to the excellent accepts the challenge of the best instead of the mediocre and questionable. It is almost as though Paul is saying, Go ahead, try it. Let it prove its value to you.

EXCELLENCE LIBERATES

Admittedly our flesh may rebel at the thought of limiting our lives to the excellent. It seems too restrictive. If we respond like that, however, we demonstrate that we have misunderstood true liberty. Our cultural concept of liberty claims that freedom is being able to do what we want to do. In reality that leads to bondage. Those enslaved by substance abuse and those in the chains of guilt all started by becoming "free" to do what they wanted to do. Doing what we want to do is a prelude to the captivity of lust and obsessive habit patterns. Christ's view of freedom is quite distinct. He teaches us that "the truth will set you free" (John 8:32). In His terms freedom begins with restriction. Restricting our lives to those things that are in the context of truth releases our spirits to be free from guilt, worry, fear, and enslaving habits. It releases us to the freedom of joy, peace, and a clear conscience.

In fact, restricting our lives to that which is excellent pays four key dividends in our lives. Philippians 1:10-11 describes the results of excellent choices in terms of a clear conscience, a blameless reputation, a fruitful life, and an existence that brings glory to God. The text moves like dominoes stacked on end. The fun way to play dominoes is to set them up on edge in a zig-zag line, tap the first domino over, and watch them fall. Grammatically, the result clauses in the two verses move just like that. An excellent choice becomes the first domino, and once it is made, the others automatically fall in place.

There are few things more valuable than a *clear conscience*. A clear conscience releases us from the fear, worry, and anxiety that comes with sin. It keeps us from paranoia, and it enables us to relate to God unhindered, without shame. The text calls it purity (Philippians 1:10). It is that inner sense of being clean. Nestea Iced Tea used to run a television ad depicting a golfer struggling up the fairway on a hot, humid day. A bag on his back, he is perspiring and completely wrung out. Then he hears the clicking of ice cubes in a glass and the sound of iced tea being poured over the ice. He is mesmerized. He drops his bag and runs to an adjoining backyard where a party is being held. He reaches for a glass, lifts it, drinks, and as he does, lost in abandon, he falls back into the swimming pool. He rises from the swirling bubbles smiling, obviously clean and refreshed. Then the words "Take the Nestea plunge" blaze their way across the bottom of the screen. I felt totally refreshed just watching it.

Philippians 1:10-11 calls for us to take the excellent choice plunge; to run from the choices that lead to a muggy and dirty interior to the refreshing, cleansing plunge of choices that produce purity.

Excellent choices also produce *blamelessness* (Philippians

1:10). A friend of mine who was struggling with a sin problem said that whenever his particular sin came up in social conversation or was mentioned in a sermon he felt like a spotlight had been beamed on h'm, exposing his sin. He was not blameless. It is a terrible thing to live with guilt and know that you are not above reproach. Guilt causes us to become critical, dishonest, fearful, and sometimes angry and bitter. An excellent choice will protect us from the liability of blame from others. It will keep fingers from pointing our direction and will cause us to be above reproach.

The third result of excellent choices is that we will be *"filled with the fruit of righteousness"* (Philippians 1:10). Righteousness is not a dead-end street. It is productive. It produces special results in our lives that are productive for God and that bring personal pleasure to us. The fruit of righteousness is a blessing to others as well. It is a powerful testimony to the uniqueness of Christ, who lives within us. God's Word describes the fruit of righteousness in terms of such valuable commodities as love, joy, peace, patience, kindness, goodness, faithfulness, gentleness, and self-control (Galatians 5:23-23). By stark contrast, choices that emanate from the flesh produce "sexual immorality, impurity and debauchery; idolatry and witchcraft; hatred, discord, jealousy, fits of rage, selfish ambition, dissensions, factions and envy; drunkeness, orgies, and the like" (Galatians 5:19-21).

Choosing fruit has never been one of my better skills. Melons are the toughest. I tap them, smell them, sometimes squeeze them. Invariably they are not real good when I get them home. I am thankful that bearing the good fruit of righteousness is more predictable and more controllable. A choice for the excellent produces through us a full crop of good and beneficial fruit.

The fourth result of excellent choices is a life that brings *praise* and *glory* to God (Philippians 1:10). It is important to remember that we were created to reflect His character and reality in our world (Genesis 1:26). We were redeemed to bring praise to His "glorious grace" (Ephesians 1:6). Bringing praise and glory to God is the centerpoint of our commission in this world. As the Shorter Westminster Cathechism states, "What is the chief end of man? To glorify God and to enjoy Him forever."

How do we glorify Him? Quite simply—by reflecting His nature in our lives. We have all been to the mirror. Unless it is at a circus or haunted house where mirrors are intended to distort, most mirrors accurately reflect our true condition. Our lives are intended to mirror God's love, mercy, grace, justice, righteousness, and a host of other divine realities to a world that cannot see God. We bring glory and praise to Him and reflect Him by becoming like Him (2 Corinthians 3:18). Excellent choices result in that kind of living. Lesser choices distort God's reflection and may totally deface Him before a watching world.

DISCERNING THE EXCELLENT

For some of us, striving for excellence will seem like an impossible task. While it may be the perfectionist's delight, it will be a burden to the "Well, nobody's perfect" crowd. But it is a burden only to those who fail to understand what a clear and simple process it is to discover the excellent choices.

God tells us, "This is my prayer that your love may abound more and more in knowledge and depth of insight so that you may be able to discern what is best" (Philippians 1:9-10). As the text states, being committed to love, knowledge, and discernment will automatically move us across the continuum of choices and land us in the excellent category. It is not a matter of arbitrarily and subjectively trying to decide what is excellent. Excellent choices are those choices that are consistent with a commitment to love, knowledge, and accurate discernment. That three-part formula provides the base from which a truly righteous life is produced. It is the key to our decision-making process.

Abounding love. The first step in discovering the excellent is a commitment to a growing love. Again love proves to be the starting point in the production of true righteousness. Because we have discovered that love is yielding to God and to the needs of those around us (Matthew 22:37-39), an excellent choice begins by asking two questions: "What would be *most* pleasing to God?" and "What would bring most benefit to those who are affected by this decision." A young business-man recently had the opportunity to take a new and better job out of state. We prayed for God to grant him wisdom. It was very tempting. He told me just the other day that he had turned it down. His reasons? First, he felt that to uproot him-self and family from the spiritual support they were getting would derail their growth in Christ. And second, he sensed that his wife and children would be shortchanged if they were taken out of an environment where friends, care groups, Chris-tian schooling, and the local church were proving to be impor-tant ingredients in their lives. His priorities of pleasing God and sensing his family's needs outweighed material considera-tion and produced an excellent choice in that setting. Time and eternity will tell what that choice will yet produce.

Knowledge of the truth. Knowledge must be added to abounding love because knowledge is the guidance factor of love. Love left alone can often be misguided and even destruc-tive. The great drift toward theological liberalism and apostasy in the thirties was often couched in terms of the pre-eminence of love over truth. The most important thing was to have a loving spirit; doctrine did not count. Much of the sensual drift of our day is a product of love without knowledge. The free-love movement operated without the knowledge that true love seeks the best for another and that unrestricted sexual liberty ushers in guilt, loss of self worth, broken relationships, hollow-ness of heart, and even physical disease. In order for love to produce excellence, it must be exercised within the boundar-ies of knowledge.

Where is such knowledge found? We should first define

where it is not found. True knowledge is not the knowledge of how I feel about something. That is far too vacillating. Nor is it found necessarily in advice from others or from our godless culture. It is found in God's Word. Recognizing that God is truth and that He has revealed truth through His Word, ultimate knowledge then is the awareness of God's truth as revealed in Scripture. There is sufficient truth in Scripture to provide knowledge for every life situation. Whereas excellence finds its *motivation* from genuine love, it discovers its *direction* from God's Word. So in our search for excellence, we add to our love knowledge.

Transients periodically stop by our church seeking financial help. It is amazing how similar all their stories sound. It would be easy to assume that they want to take advantage of the church and head right to the local pub to drink the cash away. Yet love requires us to help the poor. It is "excellent" to give a gift of love in Jesus' name to those who are in need. But it is a breach of stewardship to give a gift that will be used for the further destruction of a life. What can a church do?

First, we must make a commitment to true love in terms of helping the poor. Then we must seek knowledge.

God's Word states, "Lazy hands make a man poor, but diligent hands bring wealth" (Proverbs 10:4). That is the answer: knowledge guides love into the arena of the excellent. Love can sometimes be blind. Knowledge helps it find its way.

Depth of insight. The third step toward excellence is the ability to discern the application of the "love-knowledge" combination. Love and knowledge align us for excellence; discernment provides a wise application of what love and knowledge dictate.

For the businessman who turned down the out-of-town job, knowledge had dictated the priority of both spiritual and family values (Luke 12:31-35; Ephesians 5:25-6:3), and discernment called on him to stay in town.

Once we realized that vagrants in need should use diligent hands to gain wealth, our church began to offer small jobs for those who came asking for a handout. It was excellent! Many refused to work and walked away. They were not truly in need. Others gladly worked, preserved their self-worth, and received from their labor.

Excellence Applied

The righteous results of excellence naturally flow out of our lives as we add to our commitment to love God and others the knowledge of God's revealed word and a wise application of love and knowledge to any given situation. Again, the application of the principle begins at the centerpoint of our surrender to Christ. Excellence is outward proof of our first love for Him. It is the heat from the flame within.

Being a pastor means that I am often with people. I love it. I am a "people person." I find people stimulating, challenging, and often fun. In spite of that, I have come to realize that "people people" sometimes get peopled out. Frankly, there are times when I get in my car and head for home after a people packed day and look forward to solitude. I rejoice until I realize that there are also people at home!

I would like to head straight for a closet and ask Martie to slide supper and the newspaper under the door and not bother me for three hours. At least I should be able to read the paper and watch the news in peace. That would be a *good* choice. It helps me unwind, and if I am up on the news my ministry will be more relevant.

But I find myself thinking about the excellent. What would my Lord want me to do? How could I love Him as I walk through the door? What do my wife and children need? How can I apply love to my family? What knowledge does God give me in His Word and how would I apply it?

As I move through the excellence process I begin to realize that loving God means to love my family. I am thankful that my wife treasures my time and attention. Our fellowship means a lot to our relationship. I remember when our children were preschoolers. All day long Martie talked baby talk and wiped noses. She was ecstatic when I came home. I used to think it was me. Actually, anything over five-foot-eight and breathing would have evoked the same response.

I think of loving my children. They look forward to the time we spend together. Sending them off as I walk in the door would not be an act of love. I have always been amazed at how significant playtime is to them. Matthew wept all the way home from the airport as I flew overseas. Unable to be comforted, he finally said to his mom: "But if his plane crashes, who will wrestle with me?"

The *knowledge* of God's Word drives the point deeper. Ephesians 5:25 says, "Husbands, love your wives, just as Christ loved the church and gave himself up for her." Ephesians 6:4 encourages me to love: "Fathers, do not exasperate your children; instead, bring them up in the training and instruction of the Lord." The Lord spends time with us to suit our every need; in like manner, my children, if they are to be instructed in the ways of the Lord, need to see that reality in and through me.

Discerning the application is relatively easy in this case. I know what I must do. I walk through the door, past the closet, past the couch, past the paper, and right to the kitchen where Martie is fixing supper. "How was your day?" The words are easy. Listening carefully to her takes more discipline. I find myself hugging the kids as the youngest climbs up my body.

The ancient Seneca wrote, "Life is like a play. It's not the length, but the excellence of the acting that matters."

10

Guaranteed to Last:
The Principle of the Kingdom

It was absolutely amazing. I was in West Africa—Timbuktu
to be exact—and the missionaries were telling me that in that
culture the larger the women were the more beautiful they
were thought to be. In fact, a young missionary who had a
small, trim wife said that the nationals had told him she was a
bad reflection on him—he obviously was not providing well
enough for her. A proverb in that part of Africa says that if
your wife is on a camel and the camel cannot stand up, your
wife is truly beautiful.

How different their perceptions are from ours. We sweat,
toil, and deprive ourselves to stay thin. It is like two different
worlds. For them, fat is where it's at; for us, thin is in. It is a
matter of values. And in that part of Africa, American values
made me unique.

As Christians, our values make us unique. We live in a world
whose values are decidedly different from ours. We are people
of Christ's kingdom (Colossians 1:13), and that means that we
live by unique standards. In reality we are aliens in a foreign
place (John 18:36). As such, we, the people of the kingdom of
Christ, live not by the rules of this cosmos but by the righteous
values of Christ, the advanced principles of the age to come

(Revelation 21:1-5; 2 Peter 1:4, 17-25; 2:9-12).

CHRIST'S CALL TO KINGDOM VALUES

To a nervous, anxious group of disciples who were distracted by earthly, temporal values, Christ made a dramatic declaration.

> And why do you worry about clothes? See how the lilies of the field grow. They do not labor or spin. Yet I tell you that not even Solomon in all his splendor was dressed like one of these. If that is how God clothes the grass of the field, which is here today and tomorrow is thrown into the fire, will he not much more clothe you, O you of little faith? So do not worry, saying, "What shall we eat?" or "What shall we drink?" or "What shall we wear?" For the pagans run after all these things, and your heavenly Father knows that you need them. (Matthew 6:25-32)

The disciples were so concerned with things that were of temporal value in this world that they were distracted from the more valuable realities of the kingdom. Perhaps Peter had been talking about leaving Christ to go back to fishing because he was hungry or because his robe was wearing thin.

In the face of the distraction of temporal, earthly values Christ's conclusion was clear. "But seek first his kingdom and his righteousness, and all these things will be given to you as well" (Matthew 6:33).

Translated into the dialect of my existence, it simply means that I am to place promotion of and participation in the kingdom of Christ as a priority in my life.

What does it mean to seek first the kingdom? First, we must understand the essence of the "kingdom." At the very core of the kingdom is the reality of eternity. One kingdom truth that Christ hammered home was that there is something significant beyond the grave. It was a fact that altered His view of this life. In Christ's perspective, it made little sense to live life investing only in things that you could not take with you. He had a point. I have been to many funerals and I have yet to see a Brinks truck or a U-Haul following the hearse. As an old Spanish proverb says, "Shrouds have no pockets." Christ taught that in this life we should live so as to make a difference in eternity.

Just a few verses before His call to the priority of kingdom things, Christ had underscored that aspect of the kingdom by saying, "Do not store up for yourselves treasures on earth, where moth and rust destroy, and where thieves break in and steal. But store up for yourselves treasures in heaven, where moth and rust do not destroy and where thieves do not break in and steal. For where your treasure is, there your heart will be also" (Matthew 6:19-21). Someone has paraphrased well that statement of Christ by saying, "You can't take it with you, but you can send it on ahead."

Quite simply, Christ is commanding us to place things of eternal significance at the top of the list of what is most important in our lives. In the terms of the kingdom, which lasts forever, things that are eternally secured are to be the priority investments of life. If the kingdom had a national hymn, the theme of it would have to be something like, "Only one life, 'twill soon be past; only what's done for Christ will last."

It is really a matter of perspective. Where do we place the significance of a new car, a great career, personal comfort, a tranquil life, a dynamite romance, or anything else that is subject to time and decay? How do we view those things in contrast to the value of a soul, a life given to world missions, a third-grade boys Sunday school class, time with our families, or even the trauma and loss that is often associated with standing up for righteousness? Christ underscored the significance of our perspective on life when He said, "The eye is the lamp of the body. If your eyes are good, your whole body will be full of light. But if your eyes are bad, your whole body will be full of darkness. If then the light within you is darkness, how great is the darkness!" (Matthew 6:22-23). If we do not see the priority of the kingdom, of treasures in heaven, we are living in great darkness.

TREASURES FOR THE KINGDOM

Essentially, the principle of kingdom values demands that all of life, every decision, be weighed and measured by its eternal impact. Christ in His call to kingdom values cites specific applications of kingdom choices in terms of our treasures (Matthew 6:19-21). The word translated "treasure" is a broad word for things of personal value. As I search through the treasure chest of my own life I find items like time, talents, family, friends, money, and even some material things that are precious to me. What I must ask myself is, Do I have any treasures in heaven?

Two questions are crucial at this point. First, What are treasures in heaven? They would be things done in our life that have impact into eternity. For instance, God's Word speaks of people whom we have helped and have won to the Lord as friends who will welcome us to heaven (Luke 16:9). Eternal gain through ministry to others is seen as fruit credited to our account in heaven (Philippians 4:17). The Bible tells of rewards that await us in heaven as compensation for our faithful contribution to the kingdom of Christ. Treasures in heaven are things of eternal worth.

Second, we must ask, How do I establish treasures in heaven? Well, not by scrapping all our treasure on earth, although that may be necessary at times, but rather by investing our earthly treasures in such a way as to enhance eternity. God has intended that the temporary things of this world be used to accomplish eternal gain. That is quite different from the world's perspective which portrays things as items to be used for our own gain and glory.

In what ways can we use our treasures for eternal gain?

TIME

There are few things quite as valuable as time. For most of us spare time is a rare commodity, yet all of us are the ultimate masters of our schedule. Time can be used to invest in the kingdom: time to cultivate a relationship with an unsaved friend; time to read the Word as a family; time to pray alone; time to prepare, teach, and disciple; time to come apart and rest so that there might be strength for another day to be effective for Christ; even time for the expression of love and care that makes a difference. I was surprised recently to receive this letter about a brief moment invested in a person's life.

> Dear Pastor:
> Just a moment of your time as I know what a precious commodity it must be for you.
> I've been attending HPBC these past few months in an effort to resolve some important conflicts taking place within my life. I'm happy to say that much has been gained through each service which I've had the opportunity and privilege to attend. This is great, but unfortunately sometimes it seems the more one makes a concerted effort to draw nearer to the Lord, the more the Enemy works in a type of spiritual battle to discourage and stifle the blessings gained.
> As I sat in Sunday school this morning such a spiritual battle was raging within me. I silently prayed for some type of assistance to help overcome the negative thoughts and feelings which were overtaking me. As I left church this morning I was met with a nice surprise; a warm genuine smile and several important words, the right words, from someone who I know could have been legitimately preoccupied with more important matters than that of greeting a lone parishioner exiting from church.
> Thank you, Pastor, for taking time and making the effort to smile and speak those few simple words of encouragement as you made your way to the 11:00 o'clock service, for they worked wonders in dispelling those negative feelings which seemed quite overwhelming just several minutes prior!
> Wow, what an important lesson I learned! To think of the potential power within perhaps just a smile, a warm, firm handshake, or a couple of kind, gentle words to another

brother or sister. If we would only make the time and put forth the effort. And that's the secret isn't it, a little time and effort on our part.

Time to let you go, but let me just say thanks again for being open and sensitive to allow the Almighty to work through you. I was truly encouraged and blessed by you today and the lesson I learned I know will prove to be most important in the future. Keep up the good work!

A Christian brother

Time flies and although there does not seem to be much of it, how important it is to invest what there is in things that last forever.

CHILDREN

Among our most precious assets are the children God has given us. Unfortunately, we seem more interested in feeding them well, dressing them smartly, and educating them property than we do in instilling kingdom values in them. At the risk of overstatement, let me say that our children are often spiritually victimized and abused by our insensitivity to the priorities and values of the kingdom of Christ.

God's Word instructs us to rear our children in the "training and instruction of the Lord" (Ephesians 6:4). We do that not only through teaching them and taking them to church, but also through our example before them. Kingdom-oriented parents set a great pace for children to value the priorities of the kingdom. World-oriented parents often produce world-oriented people for the next generation.

Where are the parents who so value eternity that they would count it a high honor to have their child become a missionary, pastor, or some other calling of career ministry? It seems that many parents today want "more than that" for their children. Perhaps some of us do not want to tell our friends whose children are attending prestigious universities that our child is going to a Bible college or seminary. Some parents want to live out their own worldly dreams through their children's lives. We must remember that children are not meant to be extensions of our "wish list." God wants them to be an extension of His almighty arm. Granted, a child moving into a secular profession can have great impact for Christ if his values are right. The rub comes in those homes where parents would discourage their child from seeking an investment in career ministry.

Gratefully, prayerfully, and carefully placing our children in the treasure chest of the kingdom of Christ by loving and living kingdom values is our highest responsibility and most profound privilege. What better way is there to express our love for Him than through our children?

MONEY

Let us be honest. Money is important to most of us. It is the one thing that brings the *power* to buy, accumulate, gain status and prestige, establish security, and provide pleasure and leisure. Money is like lust: it is a wonderful servant and a terrible master. In fact, Christ taught that if money controlled us, we could not submit to God as Lord (Matthew 6:24). Simply said, if our heart is bent on loving the Lord then we can never fall in love with money, for it will become our master.

Yet money can become a powerful investment in kingdom realities. I like to think that just as Christ changed the water into wine, so He takes our silver and gold and transforms it into things that remain. The wise men gave their treasures of financial worth to the Christ child, and it financed a trip to Egypt where the Messiah would be safe from a raving Herod. So, too, we can invest our money for fruit that remains (Philippians 4:10-19).

, How much? All of it!

Christ taught in His stewardship parables that all that He gives us is really His and that we will be held accountable for it (Matthew 25:14-30). That truth is certainly a step beyond the normal "10 percent for God and 90 percent for me" formula. In fact, that limited view of stewardship actually makes us vulnerable to letting the 90 percent become master of our lives. How do I invest it all for Him? By measuring every expenditure in the light of His kingdom and eternal perspectives.

For instance, we live in a delightful neighborhood where many of our neighbors do not share our faith in Christ. Most of them know that I am a minister. I know that they watch us and the testimony of Christ is at stake. So I spend money to adequately clothe my children. We live in an area where no one has dandelions. I spend money on weed and feed so that the Christian on the block isn't the one to reseed the neighborhood lawns with dandelions. We buy groceries so that our children know that God supplies their needs.

It is important as well to keep indebtedness in check so that we have financial freedom to give directly to God's work through the local church and other worthwhile efforts in the kingdom. Not just 10 percent, that would be the minimum, but rather 12, 15, 20 percent or more. As God's Word says, we are to give in proportion to how He has prospered us in order to make friends for the kingdom (1 Corinthians 16:2; Luke 16:9). In fact, money is what God uses to test our trustworthiness and commitment to Him. As Christ said, "Whoever can be trusted with very little can also be trusted with much, and whoever is dishonest with very little will also be dishonest with much" (Luke 16:10).

GIFTS AND TALENTS

God has created us with certain talents, and at salvation He has given us special gifts to be used in the advancement of kingdom work. Yet in many cases we've allowed the kingdom of Christ to become more like a football game: twenty-two men killing themselves on the field for the cause while 100,000 sit in the stands stuffing themselves with food, socializing, cheering, and booing. One of our greatest assets for kingdom investments is the asset of our abilities. Whether it be hospitality, helping, giving, administration, mercy, music, teaching, comforting, evangelizing, or encouraging, each ability influences others in terms of eternity when done in the name of Christ and as an expression of our love for Him.

I pastor a church where literally hundreds of believers without pay and at sacrifice of their schedules and energy invest themselves in the kingdom cause. Only eternity will tell what it has meant in the lives of thousands of people, not only here but around the world.

Giving ourselves means climbing out of the stands and getting into the warfare on the field. It means giving the treasures of our abilities as a gift of love to God. Ralph Waldo Emerson said it well: "Jewels and rings are only excuses for gifts. The only true gift is a portion of thyself."

WORKING IN THE KINGDOM

Essential to kingdom involvement is not just *what* we do but *how* we do it. Kingdom work must consistently reflect kingdom values. Values such as truth, integrity, justice, fairness, purity, and righteousness must be the tracks on which the kingdom moves. Too often well-meaning Christians have tried to operate in the kingdom according to the standards of the world. Christ's work is not empowered by Madison Avenue techniques, fancy words, or clever schemes. It is energized by the Spirit's power. Expedience, manipulation, deceit, and "political" moves only derail and discredit God's work. Good soldiers do not march to the orders of the enemy's general. They take their marching orders from the cadence of their own drums. It must be that way in the kingdom.

Foundational to the way we work in the kingdom is our identity as *servants*. The disciples could not seem to grasp the fact that there were no big shots in the kingdom—only servants. They often debated about which of them would be "greatest" in the kingdom. Christ clearly charted the essence of the kingdom attitude when He reproved the disciples who were divided over power and prestige by saying,

> You will indeed drink from my cup, but to sit at my right or left is not for me to grant. These places belong to those for whom they have been prepared by my Father. . . . You know that the rulers of the Gentiles lord it over them, and their high officials exercise authority over them. Not so with you. Instead, whoever wants to become great among you must be your servant, and whoever wants to be first must be your slave—just as the Son of Man did not come to be served, but to serve, and to give his life as a ransom for many. (Matthew 20:23-28)

Very simply, yet profoundly, that means that we are here to be servants of God and of our brothers and sisters in Christ. Power plays, status-seeking, name-dropping and name-promoting, climbing ecclesiastical ladders, self-promotion, and a host of other manifestations of worldliness are not how we work in the kingdom. We invest our treasures as servants, wanting only to be meaningful into eternity and waiting for that grand day when we hear the divine compliment, "Well done, good and faithful servant!" (Matthew 25:21).

EARTHLINGS ANONYMOUS

Exercising the kingdom principle unto righteousness in our lives may mean some withdrawal. Most of us have been saved from hell but not from this temporal place called earth. Our roots have grown deeply into material things and earthly values. Our perspectives are jaded and often wrong. Becoming a true kingdom person will take a concentrated effort to love God by thinking, acting, living, and investing all that we are in the context of the real and precious worth of the kingdom of Christ.

We have all kinds of support groups to help people escape the traps in which they are caught. There is Alcoholics Anonymous, Gamblers Anonymous—I recently read of a Fundamentalists Anonymous run by unbelievers to assist young people in escaping their heritage without guilt. A California career woman recently started a Superwoman Anonymous for those women who wished to escape the rat race of the career person, homemaker, mother, wife, and lover syndrome.

Well, I have a new group that desperately needs to be formed in the Body of Christ: Earthlings Anonymous. This group would claim Christ as King over all they are and have. They would disavow the fleeting and damaging influences of this condemned world and call themselves servants as they live by the values and the ethics of the kingdom. They would sing with conviction:

> Only one life to offer,
> Take it, dear Lord, I pray;
> Nothing from Thee withholding,
> Thy will I now obey;
> Thou who hast freely given
> Thine all in all for me,
> Claim this life for Thine own
> to be used, my Savior,
> Ev'ry moment for Thee.
>
> (Avis B. Christiansen*)

A friend of mine once said, "Joe, only two things will last forever: people and the Word of God. I've decided to invest my life in them."

He is a kingdom man.

---

* "Only One Life." Copyright 1937. Renewal 1965 by Merrill Dunlop. Assigned to Singspiration, Inc. All rights reserved. Used by permission.

11

Inside-Out Righteousness: Application

An old water tank sat empty, sunken in a prison courtyard in Equador. For years it had only used to gain confessions from criminals: it was confess or drown. Now it was to be used again, but not to forcefully induce confessions. Ten known criminals would stand in that tank and voluntarily confess their sin, claim Christ as their Lord, and identify with Him in baptism.

Those men bravely expressed the very essence of authentic Christianity: a spontaneous, uncoerced love for God from the inside that unashamedly issues in a public display of righteous loyalty to Christ. Tragically, for many Christianity has moved from relationship to ritual and they have lost the freshness of spontaneity and the joy of personal love. If God had intended us to relate to Him by external actions performed because of peer pressure, He would have made us robots. The beauty of His plan is that true fellowship with Him is a relationship, expressed by a choice to love Him above everything else. Such love issues in an uncompromised expression of righteousness through the exercise of biblical principles.

INITIAL STEPS

All of us long for a sense of intimate fellowship with God. We grow tired of our ritualism; rules without relationship become burdensome. Even the best system becomes tedious without a sense of the Savior. To fan the flame of our love for Christ is the best of intentions. Yet good intentions are nothing more than vaporous dreams and wishes if they are not followed by decisive resolve and effective follow-through. Lighting the fire afresh requires several initial steps.

REALISTIC EXPECTATIONS

It is critical for us to recognize that the essence of an authentic relationship with Christ is not first of all emotional. Although the emotional dimension of our relationship with Christ is most rewarding, our "inside-out" relationship to Him is a choice to make Him the absolute priority, the reason we are what we are and the reason we do what we do. In fact, the flesh will emotionally rebel at first. Placing Christ at the core may seem threatening. It may threaten the false security of an externally motivated system. Our comfort and self-satisfaction may be at stake. The beauty of it all is that as we, by choice, make Him our first love, the emotions follow as we experience the joy and freedom of a life of righteousness that comes from within.

We may also expect that such a commitment will exempt us from temptation and trouble. Nothing could be more foreign to the essence of authentic internal righteousness. Some of God's best were tempted and tried: it is part of the fabric of living righteously in a fallen place among a fallen race. But we can expect the freshness of Christ at the core to produce power that will enable us to cope and conquer.

Nor should we expect that the commitment is a one-time, never-to-be-maintained experience. I have a friend who, when teaching Romans 12:1, says that the trouble with living sacrifices is that they keep climbing off the altar. Christ at the core is like marriage; it is not the original investment, but the upkeep that makes the difference.

Great expectations, if they are not accurate, can soon prove to be a source of great disillusionment. Expect only to place Him at the center of your life, and lovingly surrender to all that He is and all that He requires. Then let whatever comes from that commitment be your unexpected blessing.

TERMS OF RELATIONSHIP

Unhindered fellowship. First John 1 makes it clear that sin in our lives is detrimental to our fellowship with God. Stubborn rebellion is catastrophic in any relationship, and it certainly will interfere with our relationship to a Holy God. Thankfully, God does not require the purity of perfection but rather the purity of a life that is characterized by "sincerity and truth" (1 Corinthians 5:8). Sincerity is the integrity to seek the light of God to expose whatever is wrong in our lives. Truth is the acceptance of His truth as the standard for right and wrong. That is exactly David's heart when he prays, "Search me, O God, and know my heart; test me and know my anxious thoughts. See if there is any offensive way in me, and lead me in the way everlasting" (Psalm 139:23-24). The terms of an unhindered relationship simply are a willingness to have sin exposed, cleansed, and replaced by that which is true and right according to Him. As John says, "If we claim to have fellowship with him and yet walk in the darkness, we lie and do not live by the truth. But if we walk in the light, as he is in the light, we have fellowship one with another, and the blood of Jesus, his Son, purifies us from all sin" (1 John 1:6-7).

Time alone. Intimacy is developed only when there is time spent in sharing things in common. The sharing of dreams, goals, thoughts, and desires deepens and ignites the power of a relationship. It is true with our relationship to God as well. Prayer, meditation, worship, praise, thanksgiving, reading His

Word, and becoming still to know that He is God provide the groundwork for a growing sense of love for God.

DISCERNMENT

A heart for God shows its colors in our daily lives. It is measured in our attitudes, actions, and responses. Yet a heart of love for Him must operate in a hostile, alien world. The challenge of Christ is to live in that world with a wise spiritual assertiveness and a tenacious loyalty to righteousness. He said to His disciples, "I am sending you out like sheep among wolves. Therefore be as shrewd as snakes and as innocent as doves" (Matthew 10:16).

To be wise and innocent demands *discernment.* Discernment is the ability to clearly distinguish between right and wrong. It is a skill, a skill that marks us as mature believers (Hebrews 5:11-14). Discernment is an ¹internal mechanism that is not developed through external codes but rather through the discipline of a heart that applies the revealed principles of God's Word to each life setting. As such, it makes us wise and keeps us innocent.

Actually, the strength of discernment lies in the strength of the standard by which we judge life. There are many false standards that destroy discernment. Sincerity is often thought to be the most important thing in our response to life. Love, by many definitions, is considered to be the chief instrument in discernment. But neither are at the core of wise and innocent choices. Sincerity and love form the motives in discernment but are not sufficient in and of themselves. As a student, many times I answered test questions very sincerely thinking I was right—only to find later that I was sincerely wrong. Helping my child tie his shoes every morning may be an expression of love, but it will ultimately hinder him if he becomes the only college freshman in his class who does not know how to tie his shoes. Love can be well meaning but all by itself can lead us to well meant mistakes.

Sincerity and love are valuable to discernment only when they are linked to *truth*. Innocence is produced by both sincerity and truth (1 Corinthians 5:8). Wisdom can only take place when our love abounds "more and more in knowledge and depth of insight, so that you may be able to discern what is best and may be pure and blameless until the day of Christ" (Philippians 1:9-10).

The school of rational psychology charts the course of decision-making in three stages. There is first the *life situation*, which is passed through the grid of our *philosophy of life*. That philosophy of life then determines our *response* to that life situation.

The key, quite clearly, is our philosophy of life. If in our philosophy of life cats make great pets, when offered a kitten we will more than likely respond with an openness to the offer. The very same situation will elicit a "you've got to be kidding" from someone whose philosophy of life views cats as an irritation.

When our philosophy of life is built on the truth of God's principles as revealed in His Word, then righteousness, wisdom, and innocence will be the natural by-products. It is true that as a man "thinketh in his heart so is he" (Proverbs 23:7, KJV). That is exactly why the Proverbs command us, "Above all else guard your heart, for it is the wellspring of life" (4:23).

Beware, however: true discernment can be corrupted by false philosophies of life. Competing for a place in our philosophical "box" will be self, secular philosophies, cultural fads, and a host of other non-truths produced by our world. They are incompatible with truth and cannot co-exist with truth in our hearts or we will become "double-minded" and "unstable" (James 1:8).

The principles of God's Word must sovereignly reign and solely possess our hearts. They alone can establish the philosophy of life through which we produce the righteousness of Christ. God's principles become our key to discerning right from wrong. They are the standard.

THE GRID

In this book we have discussed six key principles that form a basis for discerning a biblical philosophy of life. There are more in Scripture, but these principles certainly foundational. They form a grid through which we make righteous choices. When we are committed to them we respond to all of life's situations with an inside-out, spontaneous, uncoerced righteousness that expresses a heart aflame for God. Personal ownership of a biblical philosophy of life makes detailed codes unnecessary and sharpens our ability to mature in discernment.

When faced with a particular life situation the six principles provide guidance and produce discernment. We should carefully weigh every event by their wisdom.

1. *Loving God.* What would most accurately reflect a total, sweet surrender to God (Matthew 22:34-40)?

2. *Templing.* What would most accurately reflect the fact that God dwells in me, and what would best fulfill my responsibility as a priest at the threshold, protecting the purity of His dwelling place (1 Corinthians 6:19-20; 1 Peter 2:5)?

3. *True love.* What would be most constructive in meeting the needs of those around me, even if it involves a measure of personal sacrifice (Matthew 22:34-40)?

4. *Otherness.* What would be of most benefit to my brothers and sisters in Christ as I seek to value their welfare and the promotion of love, joy, peace, righteousness, and personal edification within the Body of Christ (John 13:34-35; Romans 14:10-15:3; 1 Corinthians 13:4-8; James 2:8-9)?

5. *Choices.* What would prove to be the excellent choice as a result of committing my life to true love based on knowledge and insight (Philippians 1:9-11)?

6. *Kingdom value.* What would be most effective in maximizing my impact on eternity (Matthew 15:19-34; Luke 12:13-40; Colossians 1:13)?

As an event is analyzed in the light of those truths, discernment and righteousness will be forthcoming. Each principle will prove to be applicable in all of life's encounters. The process demands the integrity and commitment to strip ourselves of rationalization and to pursue intensely and courageously the course that pleases Him.

NEW COVENANT JOY

The most significant reality in the pursuit of a heart for God is the reality that God has uniquely equipped us to enjoy an internal, living relationship with Him. It is the privilege of the New Covenant. To a people bound by externals, God promised a better day. Ezekiel the prophet proclaimed that the day was coming when "I will give you a new heart and put a new spirit in you; I will remove from you your heart of stone and give you a heart of flesh. And I will put my Spirit in you and move you to follow my decrees and be careful to keep my laws" (Ezekiel 36:26-27).

It was God's New Covenant promise. They would receive a new spirit within them (2 Corinthians 5:17), and they would receive God's Spirit in their new spirit to motivate them to righteousness (John 14:15-18; 16:12-15). Christ ushered in that great day when He lifted the cup and said, "This cup is the new covenant in my blood, which is poured out for you" (Luke 22:20). Although specifically applied to Israel, we have been included by God's grace in a new and better way (Hebrews 10). No longer are we governed by tablets of stone. God has written His law in our hearts (Jeremiah 31:33). No longer do we worship through external priests in a Temple in far off Jerusalem. God dwells in us, and we are priests before Him (1 Corinthians 6:19-20; 1 Peter 2:5). The New Covenant equips us for a new, joyous, internal, and intimate relationship with Christ. A return to an externalized, ritualistic form of faith aborts that special privilege and wastes the very blood-bought joy of knowing and living for Him *personally*.

Christ dramatically prophesied of the New Covenant joy on

the last day of the Feast of the Tabernacles, when the miracle of drawing water from the rock was celebrated. He stood and shouted, "If anyone is thirsty, let him come to me and drink. Whoever believes in me, as the Scripture has said, streams of living water will flow from within him" (John 7:37-38). Unfortunately, that refreshing spring of inner flowing water, that inside-out work of the Spirit, is often quenched by our unwillingness to agressively maintain an intimate relationship to our Savior and friend Jesus Christ. When that happens, we should pour ourselves out to Him.

> My eyes are dry,
> My faith is old,
> My heart is hard,
> My prayers are cold,
> And you know how I ought to be,
> Alive to you and dead to me.

> Oh, what can be done for an old heart like mine?
> Soften it up with oil and wine.
> The oil is you,
> Your spirit of love,
> Please wash me anew in the wine of your love.
>
> (Keith Green*)

---

* "My Eyes Are Dry," by Keith Green. Copyright 1978 by Ears to Hear Music, Birdwing Music, and Cherry Lane Music Publishing Company, Inc. Used by permission.